An Old Man's Rules for Hitchhiking

An Old Man's Rules for Hitchhiking

...and his tales of travel and adventure in
Mexico, the United States, Indonesia, and
other regions of the World

John A. McGlynn, Jr.

GODOWN
LONTAR

An Old Man's Rules for Hitchhiking
...and his tales of travel adventure in Mexico,
the United States, Indonesia, and other regions of the World

© 2008 Glynnspring, LLC.

Published in Indonesia
by Godown, an imprint of the Lontar Foundation
Jl. Danau Laut Tawar No. 53
Jakarta, Indonesia 10210

Printed in the United States

Layout	: Saiful Hadi
Cover design	: Oky Arfie Hutabarat
Cover photographs	: Oky Arfie Hutabarat and John H. McGlynn
Typeface	: Adobe Garamond

ISBN No.   : 978-979-25-1001-0

Contents

Editor's Note

John A. McGlynn, Jr. was not a prolific writer—though he should have been. During his six-year courtship to Anna Marie Schauf, from early 1938 until their marriage in May 1944, he kept up a steady correspondence with his beloved. An inventory of his estate after his death in 1999, brought to light a trove of almost six hundred letters, dating from the end of the Great Depression to the mid-1940s, near the end of World War II. Together, these letters contain a total of almost 500,000 words. But for John and Anna Marie, both living with their parents in the small Wisconsin towns of Cazenovia and Ithaca, respectively, the late 1930s and early 1940s was a time when telephones were a luxury. And thus their letter-writing tradition began. While John in his letters recapped his frustration at not being able to pursue a college education—the Great Depression had squashed that hope—and having to settle for the humble life of a small farmer, Anna Marie steadfastly shared the daily activities of an elementary school teacher, the weather, and her responsibilities at her parent's home.

Unable to give up his dreams of a life of greater adventure, in the spring of 1938, John decided to make a bid to gain a slot on a minor league baseball team and hitchhiked to Mississippi and Louisiana where some of the teams were training. Apparently, geographic distance heightened the importance of remaining in contact with Anna Marie, and he kept up a steady stream of letters. Perhaps it was on this first extensive, solitary journey of his that John developed the wanderlust which, as the stories in this volume show, would not fade until his own death some sixty years later. During this trip he worked as an itinerant mine-worker and field hand; he rode the rails; he spents many night in hobo camps. His experiences—so different from those he had gained as a farmboy in Wisconsin—stimulated his senses and, as his nose for a good story became more acute, he regaled Anna Marie with tales of the eccentric personalities he had come into contact with on the road, gradually winning her heart as much with his quick and wicked sense of humor as with his deep-seated ardor for her.

In 1940, during World War II, John enlisted in the army and though he persistently tried to persuade Anna Marie to marry him before his departure for base camp in Chanute Field, Illinois, she refused. With her traditional Germanic sensibilities, not only was she unsure whether this mad Irishman would make an appropriate spouse, she also had no desire to be—and God forbid that something bad should happen to John actually—one of those "war widows" the neighbors gossiped about, collecting the pension of a soldier she had spent no more than a few days with as his wife.

Eventually, after passing the requisite tests and flight exams, John was placed in the Army Air Corps where he served as a reconnaissance photographer. In the service, he picked up encoding and typing skills and his letters to Anna Marie became lengthier, more colorful, and more news-filled—though no less imbued with the passion he felt for her. Moving from one training camp in the United States to another and then, finally, to England, his words were the only means he had to prove his love for Anna Marie. To keep her heartstrings bound to him, he wrote to her almost every day.

An almost three-month hiatus in John's correspondence to Anna Marie occurred after the P-38 he was flying was shot down by German artillery in February 1944. He was ejected and landed near the banks of the Rhine River in occupied France. Though he was declared missing in action and, for a time, presumed dead (because on that very same day another John McGlynn had been killed in action), he managed to survive the ordeal, living off the land and on his wits until he finally established contact with the French underground. After his second attempt to escape, he was able to trek across the Pyrenees Mountains in the dead of night via a smuggler's pass, with the help of French and Basque nationalist guides, to the safety of a British submarine waiting for him and other evacuees at the southern end of the Bay of Biscay.

After John had recuperated and had been thoroughly debriefed, he returned to Wisconsin as quickly as possible to wed Anna Marie, which he did on May 13, 1944. At that point, his writing "career" pretty much ended. Now that Anna Marie was his wife and able to follow him to the army camps in Alabama and Georgia where he spent his remaining days in military service, until his discharge in early June, 1945, the urgency for him to write disappeared and his gift for gab reemerged.

A fast-growing family to support—eventually numbering ten children—from the insubstantial income he first earned as a small farmer and, later, as a mail carrier, kept John away from pen and paper for many years to come. What spare time he did have was spent reading histories, biographies, Shakespearean plays, and translations of the Greek and Roman classics, elements of which suffused the stories he created for his children and for his poker mates at any one of the local taverns. John gained a name in the community as a speaker and was often called on to represent the local American Legion post at ceremonial events and, of course, to speak at funerals. His May Day and Veteran's Day speeches as well as his eulogies for deceased comrades were often quoted and repeated—but, unfortunately, never written down.

During the almost fifty-five years of his marriage to Anna Marie, John Jr. maintained one tradition that he refused to abandon until his own health required that he stop: hitchhiking. Almost every summer, he would take off of work for a couple of weeks or more and make his way to parts unknown, going wherever his thumb would take him, traveling with no more than a small duffel bag to cities and sites on the North American continent that he had only read about previously. One year it might be Mexico; the next year, Alaska. Sometimes he rode the rails, as he had done as a young man, and spent his vacation in a boxcars and hobo camps. One time, he finagled his way on to a Great Lake steamer and worked as a cook; another time, he assisted an elderly couple maneuver their over sized RV through Yellowstone National Park. Most often, however, he traveled the open road, exploring Indian ruins, ghost towns, Mennonite hamlets, abandoned mines or whatever else he came across in the course of his sojourn. These trips provided the raw material for the tall tales that he would tell in the year that followed—before his next hitchhiking trip.

After John's retirement from the U.S. postal service in 1980, he continued to travel, but now more frequently by car. As he and Anna Marie aged, illness and infirmity took an especially heavy toll on Anna Marie, who suffered from Progressive Supranuclear Palsy (PSP), a Parkinsonian-related disorder, which eventually robbed her of both her mobility and her ability to speak. The couple, still living on the McGlynn family homestead, found themselves more and more confined to home. Even with the assistance provided by family members and friends, John no longer had the freedom to leave home when he wished. Worse still for him, he no longer had anyone at home to engage in quick-witted repartee. And thus, he began once more to write. He didn't write much at first–mostly notes about trips long past– but after he gave me, his son, a copy of some of his notes and asked me to "clean them up" so that he could share them with others, he discovered a new way to pass some of the hours of wintertime Wisconsin.

The four stories and one "guidebook" found herein give an inkling of John A. McGlynn, Junior's vast knowledge and keen wit. Although the writings are presented here in diary form, none of them should be seen as true autobiography. Ever and always, John liked to embroider his tales. In fact, "never let truth get in the way of a good lie," was his favorite motto. He always said that he wanted engraved on his tombstone the epitaph "Here lies John McGlynn—as usual." As his son and posthumous editor, I pray that I do service to his life's principle.

John H. McGlynn

to John and Anna Marie's grandchildren

Mexican Diary

An Introduction (of Sorts)

While looking for something in the attic the other day, I came across some notes, jotted down while on a hitchhiking trip some years ago. These I shall try to reconstruct into an understandable tale that you, my children and the future generations yet un-born, might yourselves some day might come across. And if and when this manuscript is found in some forgotten trunk, in a bot-tle, or in a cave in the arid Middle East, I hope that after it has been deciphered it will provide for you, especially my direct de-scendants, a bit of amusement, if not instruction. Should this manuscript remain undiscovered until the 28th century, it might also be a source of study and wonderment for that era's anthro-pologists, that is, if indeed the human race as we know it still exists—something I very much doubt. (By that time, in all prob-ability, all human functions will have been taken over by some super breed of computer. Thought, love, loyalty, courage and even dreams will have long before been declared superfluous and the human race devolved to the primordial ooze from which it slowly emerged some tens of thousand of eons ago.)

Some of you might remember the origins of this trip about which I write. It was August of 1975, I believe, but as my notes

1

have no coherent dating system, this chronicle will have to dispense with such exactitude. At any rate, I was still a full-time rural mail carrier and a part time farmer at the time and had found myself with more accumulated vacation time than I was allowed to carry over. I therefore suggested to Mother, my dearest wife Anna Marie — or "Annie," as I sometime, called her — that we take a leisurely drive to visit our fourth daughter, Mary, in California. Annie, however, fancied herself too busy or indispensable to the local economy and declined my offer. Snubbed by my love, the obvious action was, at least from my point of view, to hitchhike west and to return to the homestead within my allotted three weeks.

You younguns were most supportive of the idea—I think Chris and Luke, progeny numbers nine and ten, were home that summer—and Mother finally reluctantly agreed. Her reluctance was not as to my going but, having read Homer's *Odyssey*, she pictured me falling amongst thieves or, worse yet, an island full of nymphs, nymphets and sirens. What a dream! At the very least she feared it would take me ten years to return from my own Trojan War. After I convinced her that would not happen, that I would not be waylaid on that island of dreams, she took a long look at me and started to laugh. While hard on my pride, her smile was a sign of acquiescence. And so the stage was set.

The "recomposition" of this chronicle took place over the course of number of days in the Winter of 1996-1997. Many were the obstacles I encountered in its writing. First of all, my notes—if that is what one can call these disjointed scraps of paper—were incomplete, and periodically I would find a page or two missing. The first time this happened I was forced to give the problem long and hard thought. What was I to do? Eventually I saw that there were but two possible courses of action: the first being to reach into my rather vivid memory and, as near as possible, reconstruct the missing section in order to give my tale a modicum of coherence; the second being to forget the whole blasted project entirely (which might have been the far wiser course).

I also saw that my decision would be affected by a two variables, the first of which was the weather. If the weather was fair why in the world would I chose to sit in the basement scratching notes on paper when I could be outside with a chain saw cutting wood or at a pub in the village playing euchre? The second variable was the condition of Annie's health, an up-and-down kind of thing that sometimes requires my presence more than others.

I went outside to check the weather and found it getting colder. Annie, meanwhile, was in fine skin and feeding. Thus, as there seemed to be no resolution of my dilemma—It's odd, isn't it, that the less urgent a decision, the more difficult it seems to be? —I decided to give myself a couple hours before making a decision. Meanwhile, I would resort to my last, but most effective, decision-making method: to place a CD on to play—Beethoven is most appropriate for weighty decisions—descend to the basement, and crack a pan of hickory nuts. If that too failed I would then consult the one true oracle whose never-failing words of wisdom are to be found in the better part of a six pack of beer.

Hours passed but in the end the signs were clear: Beethoven, the beer, and the thermometer—that day it was minus five degrees Farenheit and still dropping—as well as common sense indicated that I should return to my scribbling. And that is just what I did.

After packing a small but sturdy traveling bag with nothing but essentials and stashing my limited funds (less than $250) in various parts of my apparel and a small portion in my bag, I set out from Glynnspring and headed west, trusting my sturdy thumb to guide me to my destination and St. Christopher or whomever is the patron of nutty wanderers to watch over me on my way. The thumb worked rather well but the blasted saint looked upon me with blind eyes.

As expected, because there are no large main roads in the area, the first lap of my hike consisted of numerous short rides. Eventually, however, I arrived in, or near, La Crosse, Wisconsin, and there committed a cardinal sin of the hitchhikers bible: I accepted a ride from a jolly young couple with a new baby. (Come to think of it, damned few young couples beget used babies!) The mistake was that I went too far with this charming young couple and wound up in downtown La Crosse, a full mile from westward-heading Highway 18 and a full three miles from US I-90, my intended westerly route.

Blame my greed for extra miles and an inadequate map study, the situation was, I know, one of my own making. Unfortunately, there was nothing for me to do except to walk, a nasty word for a veteran hitchhiker, first to the Mississippi and thence west.

This demeaning chore I did perform and then almost immediately I committed an even worse transgression against the sacred commandments of hitchhiking, something one must never ever do: I accepted a ride with a drunk. Worse yet, there were two drunks in the car and, as if to add insult to injury, one was a female with long, stringy, and very dirty hair (yet another kind of person to avoid regardless of whether he or she be drunk or sober). But the long and short of it was that I had sinned and must atone for it.

This mangy pair was obviously on the run from somebody as they scanned every side road and continually looked out the back window. I suspect they were on the run from a vengeful husband or "boyfriend"—more likely the latter as nobody would be fool enough to actually marry that stringy haired strumpet. I kept telling them I had to get off at the next intersection to visit my dying grandmother, but to no avail.

After about two hours of this educational wandering on back roads, the male greaseball exclaimed, "Jesus, we're God damn near out of gas!" To which I, with unwanted generosity, did reply, "No worry. Stop in the next town and *we'll* fill up, but right now I need a drink. I'll buy."

The next town we came to was a small one, consisting of two filling stations, three taverns, one store, a small bank, a tiny post office, and one small and weather-beaten church, obviously abandoned some years before.

The lousy greaseball pulled into the alley behind the taverns. (I do believe he was much more used to parking in back lots than on main streets.) We then dismounted our weary and probably stolen steed and strode, or rather staggered, through the back door of a very seedy saloon. I carried my bag with me, saying off hand that I didn't want it stolen.

On entering the saloon, I called in a centurion voice, "We need a drink." When the balky, bald-headed baboon behind the bar detached himself from a soap opera long enough to say, "Waddayawan?" my two ridees made a bee line to the rest room. I then put a dollar bill on the bar and quickly left the place, going out the seedy saloon's front door and proceeding into the neat

5

and friendly tavern directly next door. There I ordered a beer and fell into conversation with a friendly young farmer. On learning that I hoped to get back to Highway 18, he ordered us both a beer and said, "Drink up. I'm going up to the crossroads."

My ridee was a very nice young man whose hands were work-worn before their time. He wore sturdy work shoes and neat and well laundered work clothes. I noticed in the bag of groceries on the seat between us a box of Pampers, a bag of miniature candy bars, and a new typewriter ribbon, all evidence of a solid and hardworking son of the soil.

At the crossroads I immediately got a ride to the west with a very young-looking seminarian who was on his way home to do some cadet preaching at his parent's church. He was a nice and intelligent young man, but one poor devil whom I fear will never develop a thirst for adventure. His home was fifty or sixty miles down the road and somewhere along the way he let it be known that his aunt and uncle let rooms by the night. "Sounds good to me," I said to him and when we arrived in his hometown I was installed in an immaculate upstairs bedroom at the home of his aunt and uncle, a semi-retired middle-aged couple. The three beds in my room were formerly occupied by the couple's three daughters who were now grown and gone. This, with a television, a slightly-used morning newspaper, and breakfast was $8.00.

In thinking of my misadventures that day, I will admit once more that they were all my fault for I had transgressed the holy commandments of hitchhiking; even so, I would like to point out that my desire to detach myself from my two inebriated bene-factors was in no way connected to any fear or disapproval of them. In fact they generated a sort of pitying friendship but were, nonetheless, on the run from something or somebody. I could envision the headlines in the local papers if "we" had been cornered: "Highly Respected Elderly Citizen Slain in Iowa Love-Triangle Shoot Out," or "Heroic Pot-Bellied Deputy Cracks Car Theft Ring by Shooting Aged Mail Carrier in Back—He Must Have led a Double Life." Neither headline is the kind of valedictory that you or I would like, I should think.

At any rate, the day had ended well as I was then about to bed down in most pleasant surroundings with most pleasant hosts. Before falling to sleep I promised myself that on the morrow, when heading westward on the open road, I would strictly obey all the rules of hitchhiking laid down by the ancient prophet—namely, me.

I awoke in the morning, thank the Lord, and after my goodly landlady called up the stairs, "Ready for breakfast?" I partook in an old fashioned farm breakfast of coffee, juice, large patties of pork sausage, and pancakes, liberally laced with butter, locally-grown sorghum and prayer. Thereafter I went back to the open road, heading west to bypass Omaha, a veritable rattrap for hitch-hiking, from where I would go south to Kansas, and then west again.

My first ride, which took me one hundred miles to Central Nebraska, was with a most uncommunicative man, a retired high school teacher. The landscape was rich with agricultural providence—about fifty percent corn, twenty-five percent soybeans, and twenty-five percent cattle pasture—but, after four or five hours, started to become almost as monotonous as the driver. Saying that, however, after some miles, he did loosen up a bit, though not by very much.

The man had never in his life been outside the states of Iowa and Nebraska, not even in his forty odd years as a teacher. I felt sort of sorry for the bugger, he being so totally without curiosity, but he provided a lengthy ride and delivered me to a primary intersection about one hundred miles southwest of Omaha.

As it was about noon at that time and there was a small truck stop and tavern across the way from where I was dropped off, I entered the establishment, intending to buy myself a sandwich, and there fell into conversation with a large man who positively exuded good nature. This jolly fellow seemed to know everybody that came in, and they all knew him. At one point "Red," as that's what one and all called him, said to me: "I see you're hitch-hiking. I can take you hundred-fifty two-hundred miles if you wish." That was exactly what I wished, especially in view of the man's apparent joviality.

Red informed me that we would have to make a few stops on the way but that we would get to his home town before dark. I asked if there was a motel in his town and he assured me that a good friend of his had an old hotel, one that was good, clean, and cheap. "It's usually rented out to harvest or construction crews, but it's slack time right now, so Jake should be able to fix you up with something. Besides, Jake has the best damned restaurant in south Nebraska downstairs."

My ride with Red proved to be one of the most enjoyable I have ever had. His "few" stops turned out be at least twenty or more and during our trip it was revealed that Red and his "cor-poration" controlled practically the entire distribution system for beer and snack foods in the southern half of the state. Red's stops were part of a goodwill tour of his numerous customers who, without exception, welcomed him with trust and affection and called him by name "Red."

We discovered that we were both veterans, both products of

the Great Depression, both former farm boys, and both graduates of very small country high schools. Thus, in spite of the numerous stops, the day went by both quickly and pleasantly. Red didn't volunteer much info about his business, but it was obvious from the atmosphere that greeted him at all of the stops we made that he was well liked and highly regarded.

Among the papers scattered about in Red's car I noticed stationery with the logo "R&J Corporation." When I casually asked about the size of his company, Red released one of his infectious guffaws and remarked, "The last time I checked, the other half of the company weighed about one hundred forty-five pounds. 'R' stands for 'Red' and 'J' for 'Jody.' We were incorporated with papers of elopement."

It was around this time that we drove into Red's hometown — "Population 2222" — which, Red claimed, was the largest and friendliest town within one hundred miles. I soon became convinced that his claim was true.

Red announced that he would help me get me settled at Jake's "emporium" before he went home and he drove up to and parked outside a restaurant, the only one on Main Street. We walked in and Red went back to the kitchen area and yelled, "Hey, Jake, I've got a pleasant-looking white-haired man in immaculate white."

Red introduced me to Jake and I inquired about a room. Jake pointed to the stairs and quipped, "There's three or four empties up there. Take your choice." When I asked about the rate and a key, he said, "See what it's worth to you. As to the key there might be one around but I don't need it if you don't."

Red was just about to leave when he turned to me: "Damned near forgot it, John, but tonight is the beer and B.S. meeting down at the American Legion clubhouse. We'd be honored if

you'd join us. Usually starts about 8:30. Gotta go. See you there."
And out went my new friend Red.

As Jake was needed in the kitchen, I betook myself up the stairs to inspect my digs and found them to be very satisfactory. In its heyday the establishment had been a hotel for railroad crews, but now the rooms were largely rented out to transient cattle buyers and the like, and, sometimes, even an elderly hitchhiker.

The hour indicated that it was time for a bit of food and, with my room being directly above the "best damned restaurant in the state," I proceeded down the stairs to Jake's eatery. A well-run place it turned out to be. Jake, who was head cook, was assisted by two full-time and one part-time helpers. His wife kept an eye on everything out front, including the till, the restaurant's three waitresses—all charming and efficient lasses—and one busboy. The food was ample and delicious.

Mrs. Jake found time to come talk a bit. I told her the town seemed to be a friendly place and she said, "Yes, it is. Anyway, you came in with Red, and any friend of Red and Jake is a friend of everybody. Hope you enjoy the old goat's beer and BS session."

As it was then 6:30 P.M. I decided to look over the town before going to the Legion Hall. The town was what one might say in a state of "masculine disarray" but I did manage to locate the hall, site of Red's beer-and-BS session. As it was only 7:00 P.M. there were few people in the hall and I struck up a conversation with the clean-cut bartender by the name of Jeff. When I told young Jeff that Red had invited me to a get-together he reconfirmed that a friend of Red is a friend of everybody. He also told me that his wife was a niece of both Red and his wife Jody, which would mean that a sister or brother of Red's had married a sister or brother of Jody. At any rate, Jeff regarded Red as next unto

God, maybe even a jump ahead. Red had helped Jeff start up his own business, an on-site machinery repair shop which was bustling with six full-time employees. Jeff's wife did all the book work and parts inventory control for the shop on Red's computer at no charge. This was yet another reason Jeff looked on Uncle Red with absolute awe.

Just when Jeff was beginning to wax even more poetic about Red, the door to the hall burst open and in came the devil along with "the other half of his corporation." Everyone paused to call out a welcome to one or the other R&J partner. Red then ordered beers for the three of us.

Jody, Red's wife, proved to be just as jolly as her spouse. She was a small but buxom lady of about seventy and brimming with life. At one point she slapped Red affectionately across the shoulders and said, "I have to get to that Girl Scout meeting. Don't wake me up when you stagger home."

By this time a dozen or so mostly elderly fellows had arrived. Almost as if by pre-arrangement, I was made to feel part of the group. For a time we stood around sipping our beers, talking man to man. Eventually, after another beer or two had been consumed, the evening's meeting sort of oozed into being, coming to order with a comment from Red, "Well, Dog Face, what do you think?"

Dog Face was an elderly and prosperous farmer who had acquired his nickname in grade school many years before and never been able to get rid of it. (In fact, most all of the sturdy yeoman present had monikers they had acquired at an early age and had carried on through life because, even as old men, their circle of friends remained pretty much unchanged. I learned that many, too, were at least vaguely related.) At any rate, at this signal, one and all present replenished their glasses and drew a chair to the oblong meeting table to await Dog Face's presentation.

Though rather pedantic in style, Dog Face was quite convincing when speaking of the insidious threat that corporate farming represented to the community. In summing up his speech he asked a series of rhetorical questions: "What do they care about what we've protected for three generations—our schools, the town park, the town's economy, the baseball team? Nothing! What do they really care about? Not our future, for sure, but profits for distant stockholders!"

The unspoken rule of the B.S. meeting was that when the listeners' steins were almost empty, the philosopher of the moment would sit down and purchase another round—a very democratic method, I thought. In that way a bore could be silenced merely by drinking up in a hurry. And vice versa, if the philosopher was thought to be particularly witty or profound, the steins would be drained slowly.

As to payment, the rule seemed to be for the person who was ordering the beer to toss into a cigar box whatever amount he felt like giving. Given that the beer was provided wholesale by Red and the cheese and pretzels on the table appeared as manna from heaven, there was usually a surplus left in the box at the end of an evening. I was told that whenever the surplus in the kitty reached fifty dollars, the money would be given to the local 4-H Club, the Girl Scout troop, or the baseball team – whichever group was in the most dire need.

When I awoke the next morning it was raining so I decided to remain in my small but comfortable room in order to catch up on my note-taking.

Of the subjects discussed the evening before some were great and some were small; some were inane and boring presentations, calling for quick refills of beers, but one was a rather entertaining if facetious tirade by an old and well-to-do bachelor farmer by the name of Sonny, yet another boyhood nickname.

The theme of Sonny's talk, which he delivered with a certain wry wit, was the beauty of domesticity—the patter of little feet, the joy of welcoming a son home from war, of whiling away long winter evenings beside a loving spouse, and so on and so forth.

Knowing the man's history—his bachelorhood, comparative wealth, and extreme generosity—somebody asked why in the name of God he himself had never married. Sonny, a truly gentle and witty old soul, merely answered: "The ones I'd have and the ones that would have me, the devil himself couldn't match." With that he looked at the assembled multitude and said, "Hell, you all look thirsty. Drink up!"

After Sonny had replenished our glasses the philosophers then turned to me, an expectant look on each man's face. So it was that I took the floor. All in all, it went rather well. I spoke of myself, my upbringing, my lifetime of familiarity with dairy farming and involvement in that field. I spiced my tale with some travel anecdotes and concluded with a sincere critique of our educational system.

The men's steins lowered slowly, giving me a small rush of pride. I then added that I was a third-generation born of Irish-Catholic immigrants, an animal as unknown in these climes as is the polar bear, but whose welcome by these worthy people provided clear evidence of the brotherhood of man. To bring my part of the conclave to a close, I then gulped my beer and announced, "God, I'm thirsty!" Ordering a refill for the men, I was now a full member of the club.

The last speaker at the convocation of this prairie-grove of academia was, by custom, Mule Shoe, a character with enough life-tales to fill an entire volume, a few of which I will relate later. The reason for Mule Shoe always being last was, as Red informed me, "When Mule's had too much, it's time for all of us to go home!"

At the meeting that I attended Mule Shoe held forth with great wit and wisdom. He spoke for some time of the futility of taking life too seriously, a veiled criticism of the rest of us and our lifestyles, as well as, as I now see in retrospect, the wisdom of hopelessness.

After Mule Shoe had delivered his spoof on our so-called "civilization," and as his glass was dangerously low, he solemnly announced that his "delicate health" compelled him to sit down, meaning, as Jake translated for me later, "I've had about all I can hold."

Mule Shoe's words marked the formal ending of an informal meeting, probably one of the most enjoyable, gratifying, and uplifting evenings of my lifetime. I am willing to bet that if Socrates, Plato, Aristotle, and Samuel Johnson were alive and in the vicinity they would have given at least one tooth to have been allowed to sit at the feet of Red, Jake, Mule Shoe and, with utter lack of humility, yours truly.

Around noon that day the rain began to ease and my stomach began to growl. Thereupon I went downstairs both to have a bite to eat and to converse with Jake, who had also been present at the philosophers' convention the night before. As an Air Force veteran of World War II, we found that we had a good bit in common.

Jake and I talked for a bit, but as the place was getting busy and he was needed in the kitchen, he left me with an invitation to join him at the Legion Hall later for a bit of pool or sheepshead.

As it was already 3:00 P.M., and a light rain was still falling, I decided not to leave town until morning. Nonetheless, somewhat muddled as to how I had come to be in this rather out-of-the-way town, I decided to check out the roads leading west and south out of town. Once I had done that I decided that my next destination would be Central Kansas, where there was a major highway and from where I would travel west, as far as California if time permitted.

During my foray about town I purchased a newspaper and a writing tablet at the local drug store, then returned to my room to read and write until my evening assignation at the Legion Hall.

When meeting Jake that evening, we shot a couple of games of pool and had a long and entertaining talk. Jake was well acquainted with everyone in the area and could describe them all in an uproarious manner.

Included in Jake's sketches of the local populace were lengthier descriptions of two budding Socrates who were present at the philosophers' conclave the night before. The two men, Mule Shoe and Prod, were both long-time residents of the area yet were so different from each other they might have been from different planets.

Mule Shoe, who served as a volunteer bartender was a jolly fellow and seemed to be universally liked. He himself had an insatiable thirst and he saw to it that all partially-full steins were properly drained down his throat before a new glass was drawn for his colleagues and an extra full one delivered to himself. He carried this off quite well and seemed to be treated almost like the group's mascot. Prod, on the other hand, was a reticent man and was, for the most part, pretty much ignored by the others, a situation he seemed to like.

I had intended to finish my tale of the philosopher's meeting at one straight go but, with the time for sleep approaching and a promise of better weather in the morning, I decided instead to settle my tab with Jake; I would leave town before Jake opened his place in the morning and get a good night's rest.

When I went down to pay Jake and asked him how much I should leave for the room, he told me, "Hell, I don't want anything; the place was empty anyway. But you might leave a few dollars for whomever cleans up the place." And that was that.

Two days passed before I found enough time to continue my writing. At the time I was sitting in the park of a small northern Texas town, a village of no more than a dozen buildings, waiting for a ridee to return from an errand for me. On the small table in front of me was a cooler of provisions — canned caribou and sour-dough bread, if I remember correctly — kindly left behind for me by my generous pilot. Though I will eventually come to the hows and whys and whos of this particular phase of my journey, in order to keep this chronicle in roughly sequential order, I must first return to that Nebraska hotbed of friendship and philosophy and tell you a little about Mule Shoe, who was by unspoken agreement the last budding Socrates of the informal Legion-Hall get-togethers.

Most of my information about Mule Shoe was dispensed to me by Jake, the restaurant and hotel owner, who said of him, "Hell, he's indispensable, a damned good handyman. Don't know what the biddies and kids would do without him. Besides he's the jolliest town drunk any town ever had."

Mule Shoe first appeared in the town from nowhere some twenty-five years previously and had been a fixture since. According to Jake, he was probably a "left over" from a migrant harvest crew, but nobody knew for sure and Mule Shoe himself wouldn't say. At first he had been regarded with suspicion by the townsfolk but due to the man's unfailing good nature he eventually came to be accepted and well liked.

Even if his background was a mystery, the town had a demand for his ability as an odd-job man; it is this that had brought him acceptance.

By day he worked cheerfully and for anyone, but especially the town's numerous biddies (the term Jake used for any widows), putting on storm windows, cleaning unused buildings, and doing small plumbing, electrical, and roof-repair jobs. In the process of cleaning out the houses and sheds of these biddies, Mule Shoe amassed a substantial wardrobe with some of clothes dating back to the late 1800s, with examples of every kind of fashion in between. All of his clothes were of good cut and material but wildly incongruous when used in combination. "Even so," as Jake said with a hearty laugh, "most town drunks have at least a slight odor, but not our Mule Shoe. If you can smell moth balls, it means that Mule is in the neighborhood."

Jake had a most infectious belly laugh and just telling me about Mule Shoe's wardrobe produced a paroxysm of chuckles. So infectious was his laughter I was soon chortling along with him and begging to hear more.

Jake told me that when Mule Shoe was "summoned" by some biddy for work, he would do one of two things. He would appear forthwith at the woman's house and proceed to do an excellent job or, if his thirst and his funds indicated a better way of spending the day, he would send word back to the summoning biddy through one of the town's many young teenage lads (whom, it seems, also and positively adored him), that "Mr. Shoe's delicate health indicates a later day." (All the biddies addressed him as "Mr. Shoe.")

The whole town knew what that meant, namely that he was about to set off on an alcoholic tangent. If the biddy was particularly officious, insisting that he come to her house, he would reply that he had suffered a reaction to his medication and that it would be a day or more before he could come. For Mule Shoe, the term "reaction" meant hangover. And if the biddy still persisted, then Mule Shoe would take on a different biddy's chores, thereby sending a message to the former that he would not be summoned as a servant or slave. (Generally the biddies got the message the first time.)

Another reason for Mule Shoe's indispensability to that small city was his civic-mindedness along with his contributions to the community. Jake reported that a number of years previously the city had been faced with the costly need to both repair and extend the water and sewage systems, a prospect that promised to increase the city's tax rates for many years to come. At the final city council meeting to decide on the project, there were present a lawyer, an engineer, and a representative from a bonding company who were supposed to be representing the city's interests as well as representatives of several general contractors who were there to tender bids.

According to Jake, all of those mentioned—probably, and especially, including the city's hirelings as well—were licking their

18

chops in anticipation of enriching themselves at the expense of the city's townspeople, whom these parasites regarded as yokels just ready to be hoodwinked. After the numerous official presentations that evening, Mayor Red—Yes, he was not only the city's favorite son, he was also its mayor—asked for comments from the floor. And that's when Mule rose to speak.

Now on that particular night, as Jake told it, anybody else would have come across like a damned fool, but not Mule; he was the epitome of dignity, wearing striped peg-legged trousers, pointed shoes with spats, a collarless starched shirt with a narrow silk scarf about his neck, and, on top of all that, a velvet collard and belted "smoking jacket" circa 1910—all smelling of moth balls.

On taking the floor, Mule placed his hat on the table, removed from therein a sheaf of papers, and proceeded for a half hour to present facts, figures, and alternatives, all elucidated so well and with such exactitude that the high gloss of the lawyer, engineer, and potential bidders faded to the point of invisibility. Upon seeing that there would be no critical voting that night, Mule then bowed to the mayor, and announced that his delicate health dictated that he leave. He then carefully donned his derby and departed. The end result of all of this, Jake said, was that within a week, specifications were redrawn, bids were let, and bonds were marketed. "Hell," Jake concluded, "Mule saved the town a year of hassle, and at least a hundred thousand dollars by his studies and presentation."

Given Mule's civic-mindedness, it's not all that surprising that he eventually found himself sitting on the city council, a position that he had held, when I met him, six or seven years.

As to how Mule came to be elected to the city council, that's a story in itself. According to Jake, the posting of Mule's name on the election ballot all began with the machinations of an invisible hand — probably Red's — for the city's general amusement. What happened is that one year, prior to the city council election, one of the old-guard members neglected or forgot to file his nomination papers. Learning of this, Red got some of his beer and BS buddies to circulate nomination papers for Mule Shoe. A slight glitch was encountered when they learned that Mule Shoe's legal name would have to be on the ballot. Their city council candidate was being completely non-cooperative, refusing to divulge his name but, lo and behold, the problem was solved by the rural mail carrier.

Mule Shoe maintained a postbox at his tiny but well-kept trailer at the edge of town and, according to the mail carrier, received from time to time letters from the Veterans Administration and the IRS in the name of John A. Flannery. So that was the name that appeared on the ballot, much to the chagrin and outrage of the old-guard member who had forgotten to file his papers and who was, according to Jake, a damned pompous old ass or "POA" as he called him.

As a former president of the local bank, the said POA was a firm believer in the divine right of former bank presidents. But no worry, Mule Shoe would never be elected, or so the old ass thought, who passed the word to a timid assistant bank cashier, the local lawyer, and a crusading "hard-shell" preacher, to instruct everyone to write his name in at election.

Unfortunately for the POA he had picked the three most unpopular men in town to pass the word, but he, in his sublime arrogance, assumed that his reputation would resolve the election. In a sense it did, with the final election tally showing Mule Shoe with one hundred forty votes and POA with five.

Much to the general public's surprise, but not to Red, Jake, or the rest of the Philosophical Society, Mule Shoe turned out to be one of the most thoughtful and well-informed people ever elected to the town council. I knew from my conversation with Mule Shoe that he had a fairly good formal education and had read deeply, including everything from the Sears and Roebuck catalog to Homer in the original Greek.

Before ending that story about Mule Shoe and beginning another, Jake remarked with a jolly guffaw, "I always wondered who the fifth idiot was to vote for him. I know for sure it wasn't the old fool's wife."

Jake's inimitable style of story-telling makes any written record of his tales seem but pale in comparison. Nonetheless, I would like to relate something else that Jake had to say about Mule Shoe: "Mule Shoe is," Jake told me, "the favorite of a small bunch of "DGs"—Do-gooder reformers—here in this town." When I asked Jake why, he answered, "It's simple. That type of guy needs someone to save; he needs a horrible example of humanity and Mule fits the bill perfectly. Even better for them, Mule Shoe is clean and doesn't swear. He's also reliable and not about to leave town or get thrown in jail. Thus, the DGs like to hire Mule for their odd jobs so they can pester him the live-long day with their preachments. Unknown to them, Mule totally ignores their advice, but it makes the DGs happy. Mule Shoe doesn't take himself seriously, much less those potential saviors; he's not about to let himself get reformed by one of the rival do-gooders."

Jake guffawed when he said, "I don't know for sure but I think Mule's got another card he plays on these sincere but misguided hypocrites." What Jake guessed was that after work, a nourishing meal, and prayers at the home of one or another do-gooder, Mule would casually mention to his employer-host-savior that he's going to be doing a spot of work at the home of Reverend So-and-So or some other rival DG on the morrow. Such a comment would, of course, raise the hackles of fear in that day's do-gooder. Why should he plant the seeds of reformation in Mule and let some other evangelical reap the credit? Slyly, the DG will slip Mr. Shoe an extra fiver or maybe a jug of what clearly is rot gut wine but which he describes as a bottle of grape juice that his Aunt So-and-So left him, knowing all too well that the result of his munificence will in all probability bring on an attack of Mule's "delicate health," possibly even a "reaction to medication," but thereby keeping Mule safe from the clutches and ministrations of the rival DG

It's now three days later and I am seated on the rickety balcony of a small and Spartan room that overlooks the inner courtyard of a *hacienda*—if that's what it's called—in Mexico City. Only one small hanging light bulb illuminates the room's belongings: a small and lumpy cot, a table with pitcher of water and glass, and a most ornate old chamber pot. How did I come to be there? How was I to get from there to wherever I was going? What was I going to do while I'm here? These were the questions I was asking myself, the only answer I could find for which was, "I'll be damned if I know!" But as the old Irish saying goes, "Even a rat never goes in a hole he can't get out of." I was not overly worried.

I had intended at that point in my travels and my note-taking, to bring my disjointed narrative and the tale of this old navigator up to date. There were still a few more of Jake's character sketches which, if time and opportunity permitted, I hoped to put down in written memory but as there were still a couple of hours of daylight left I thought it would be well for me to first go out and familiarize myself with the area. Long ago I learned that when billeting in a strange city it is well-advised to reconnoiter your domicile's environs in daylight. This is especially true if you find yourself in a city the size of Mexico City with some ten million souls speaking a language foreign to your own.

For the couch potatoes among my children and descendants I would like to give a little bit of traveler's advice: When you arrive in a place, first jot or put to memory both the name of a street or avenue in the neighborhood as well and the names of dominant buildings. Following that, walk a slight distance from your place of stay and look back. Note the area's landmarks—church spires, smoke stacks, distinctive tall buildings, and so on—but disregard mounds or hills as their appearance might change from different angles. Thus prepared, venture forth for a mile or so in any direction. Once you have done this and returned safely to your *casa* (or whatever we Latinos call it) you will, one hopes, have the confidence to make an unguided trip of the whole metropolitan area in the light of the first full day.

Also keep in mind that you are in a strange land and the chance of finding someone who speaks your "foreign" language might very well be slim. As such, to a great extent, you will therefore be forced to rely on sign language which, however instinctive and universal it might be, will be fairly useless in the dark. For this reason do your first scouting trip in good day light.

At any rate, I then proceeded to follow my own advice and undertook an enjoyable reconnoiter and successfully returned to my digs. During my sojourn I met several street vendors and from one purchased my evening meal: a large cup of various kinds of local fruit mixed together and a piece of semi-cremated meat on a stick—probably road-kill armadillo, but edible.

So there I was sitting on the balcony of my room looking down through the fading light at the open courtyard, wherein cavorted a great gaggle of small children, several smallish goats, and some thirty, forty or fifty scrawny roosters—fighting cocks, I assumed. I couldn't figure out who was chasing whom but one and all seemed to be having a good time.

Just about that time my landlady, a rotund, youngish-looking woman of around thirty, came to see me. In fact, at first I wasn't really sure of Ita's status, that being her name, but she seemed to be in charge when my ridee, whom I shall tell you about later, dickered to let the room to me.

I was forced to converse with that dusky pumpkin in sign language. Her total English vocabulary was confined to two words: "*peso*" and "*gringo.*" I, on the other hand was much more conversational in Spanish with three words: *mañana, señor,* and *señora.*

Even with these linguistic limitations, our conversation, if that is what it can be called, was quite enjoyable. The first thing Ita did was to call down to the tumult in the courtyard. One and all below, including the goats and chickens, listened to her, laughed, and then took up the chase again. Smart kids these, I thought. Even the very young could speak and understand Spanish.

Following a few moments of silence, after Ita had seated herself on the other end of my wicker divan, she pointed to a narrow wedding band on her ring finger and then down to the melee below, after which she held up two fingers, the obvious meaning being that two of the children below were hers. She then pointed at my wedding ring and showed me her upturned palms, an international question mark, asking me, I assumed, how many children

I had. On seeing all ten of my fingers pointing upward, she assumed an expression of disbelief but reached over, gave me several pats on the shoulder, and said, if I heard correctly, "*Bueno, Señor.*"

Dusk was gathering and dusk in those climes is a brief period, a matter of no more than fifteen or twenty minutes before the day turns from light to absolute darkness.

Ita again called down to the happy melee below and the gamins faded into the darkness and behind numerous doors. The cocks began to bed down on my balcony railing and the goats simply disappeared.

When Ita rose to go she again pointed at my ring and my hands, as if not fully convinced as to the size of my family. When once again I raised all ten digits, she finally seemed persuaded. She then flashed a dazzling smile and pointed at her ring and then at her broad belly, the apparent message being that she was soon to be a mother again. After that she waddled away in the darkness. (My use of the word "waddle" is, in Ita's case, in no way derogatory. There are various kinds of waddles: there is the sad waddle, the pitiable wattle, the hopeless waddle, but Ita's waddle was one of regal dignity, the waddle of the gods.)

Following Ita's departure I, too, decided to bed down for the night, fully expecting to be serenaded at some ungodly hour by the several fighting cocks perched just outside my open window.

Another two days passed before I found a chance to write. The opportunity presented itself at siesta time, when I found myself sitting on my butt waiting for my ride under the shade of a palmetto some forty or fifty miles east of Mexico City on the road to Vera Cruz. The character who brought me to that place, and who will in good time and in some reasonable sequence be introduced into this narrative, had apparently decided that he would rather rest than drive. As I am not a person who can easily sleep in the afternoon, I took out my pen and paper with which to write in the interim.

For the relatively brief time I stayed in that small town of population 200 in Nebraska I picked up an incredible number of stories and there's one more that I would like to tell before leaving that state and revealing how I came to be in Mexico. Like most of my other tales, this one, too, was told me by Jake. It's about Prod, one of the other fellows who participated in the philosophical conclave.

First, about Prod's name: Jake, who knew Prod well and had even been in the same grade school (though he was four years older) said that the name was a shortened form of the phrase "that damned prodigal."

Prod was an only child, born comparatively late in the lives of one of the area's wealthiest farming couples, and he had been "spoiled rotten" from day one. His Mother was convinced that her darling was some sort of superior being and had little trouble convincing Prod to think likewise.

"Hell, he got the best education of any of us," Jake reported, "but was kicked out of three good colleges by the time he was twenty. Always, according to his mother, because of somebody else's fault."

When in his early twenties, Prod found himself orphaned and the sole heir to what was for that time and place, a considerable fortune: a large wheat farm and a modest cattle operation. Prod thence set himself up as a wise young rich man, and so began a morality tale.

Prod's first mistake was to think that he could turn over all the labor for his ventures to hired help. In isolated cases that works, but rarely. Jake, for all the world sounding like an old testament prophet remarked, "Hell, he clear forgot that it's the eye of the master that fattens the cattle."

The precipitous slope on which Prod had found himself suddenly grew steeper, especially when he fell for get-rich schemes that worked well for their promoters but greased the downward slide of their investors. The problem for Prod is that his inheritance was practically all in land, equipment, and cattle. So, to participate in these schemes, Prod began to borrow money, first on a small scale, then on a larger one, through mortgages, chattel and real estate. Not to worry, he thought. One of his schemes was sure to soon bear fruit and he would be rich beyond any dreams of avarice.

The clouds on Prod's horizon began to be visible when the local banker, an old friend of Prod's family, called on him to deliver a stern lecture on the financial facts of life. What nerve, Prod thought, a small town banker lecturing a future millionaire!

Because Prod's promoters didn't like the idea of their client receiving such subversive advice they induced the sucker to go to Kansas City and see for himself how promising his investments were going to be. Besides, knowing that the poor dope hadn't as yet mortgaged the main home farm, there they could arrange such a minor detail (and henceforth pick him clean) without interference. Their only mistake in convincing Prod to take out a large mortgage from a major bank on his farm was that they also introduced him to a cast of fast women and slow horses which proved to be a siphon for Prod's pool of liquid assets.

"The poor fool didn't know what hit," Jake said. "Soon the

tone of Prod's mail from home was polite but firm. 'Sir, we remind you of overdue note' And soon after that, much firmer! 'If at least the interest of chattel mortgage is not paid, action will be taken. You are notified that on such a date, mortgage will be foreclosed and sheriff's sale will ensue.'"

This should have been the finish but Prod's parasitic friends assured him that a mere ten grand more would absolutely assure the fruition of all their schemes. How about taking out a second mortgage on the home farm? So it was, back to the Kansas City to the bank that held the first mortgage. Unfortunately for Prod and his friends, a mere ten grand wasn't enough. The bank informed him not only that no additional money would be loaned to him but, due to the fact that no interest had as yet been paid on his first loan, foreclosure proceedings had already been initiated.

Such was the end of the road for the spoiled young man who had but three years earlier been considered the richest youth in the area. On the tail of Prod's financial ruin, his "business partners" disappeared, his fast women departed at full speed, and his slow horses either stopped trotting or died.

The whole affair left Prod more than slightly confused. He, who had been raised from childhood to believe that he could do no wrong, that mistakes were always made by others, was forced to leave Kansas City owing two months of unpaid rent and taking with him nothing more than his clothes and a car. Back home all that could be salvaged from the wreckage were a few cattle that had somehow escaped from having been encumbered. These, he soon sold, too, after which he went to visit two of his old biddy kinfolk where he ended up visiting for more than twenty years.

The two ladies take care of his needs and occasionally "lend" him some money for his needs, all the while trying to assure everyone that Prod is just waiting for his investments to "mature"—knowing damned well it's a lie, of course, but as they are old ancestor worshippers and Prod is the titular patriarch of the tribe, they have no other choice.

When I asked Jake why the group of men put up with Prod or why they pretend to take him seriously, he told me, "The answer might be, I suppose, that any of us could be in his shoes if we, in our childhood, had been as utterly and completely spoiled by a neurotic mother and domineering father. But I think that the real answer is the dog-cat syndrome in us. You know practically all dogs chase cats. They don't really want to catch the cats, but they do want to feel superior to something. I don't really know, but it sort of scares me to think that the rest of us are the dogs and Prod's the cat."

Such were the last words I heard from the lips of my wheat field Socrates.

On leaving Jake's hotel that day, after some thirty-six or more enjoyable hours in that friendly burg, I walked the three or four blocks to the junction and was soon back on the road, bound for California, I thought, but this proved false, though only by about three thousand miles.

I caught my first ride almost immediately. The driver was a young high school teacher and coach, a very perceptive but rather taciturn young man who dropped me off in a tiny town on the Kansas border where I had a cup of coffee and then proceeded back to the road.

The very first vehicle, a very large and very new van with

Saskatchewan, Canada plates—*Hitchhiker's note: Always look at the ridees' plates, if at all possible.*—pulled up beside me. The van was absolutely jammed with boxes and crates, and its driver was a young lady (of twenty-two years, I later found out) who, on first appearances, seemed to be rather large and well-proportioned.... About her one must simply wax poetic.

At any rate, the young lady stopped and I climbed aboard. After the usual small talk, she told me that she was going to Mexico City, on a sort of "rescue mission." Thinking that the helpless maiden might be in need of protection, and despite the personal sacrifice involved—Mexico City is a devil of a detour if one is headed for California—I offered to accompany her. She agreed.

Later, about the time we were pulling into a filling station to refuel, I asked her if she wasn't afraid to be traveling with a largely unknown old bugger like me. She answered with a broad smile, "Not really" and, ye gods, when the young lady untangled herself from the van's large cab, I understood why. Her towering figure not only dazzled my eyes but completely awed this mere mortal. She stood six feet two inches high and weighed a good two hundred twenty-two pounds. The amazing thing is that she was so perfectly proportioned you lost awareness of her size. In my mind I immediately went back to the Great Phideas' artist's conception of the statue of the Goddess Athena. This woman would have looked perfectly at home in a temple atop Mount Acropolis and, from then on, I regarded her as the favorite daughter of the great god Zeus—and to think that I was the first mortal to travel under her care since the doughty Odysseus!

Over the course of the next few days we developed an almost father-daughter relationship. In fact, as a sign of my affection for her, I soon began to address her as Athena, while she called me,

"Little Father." Perhaps it was because of this development that she clued me into the reason for our crusade, its objectives, and the planning that went into it.

To understand the reason for Athena's mission, one must have a little historical background: Back in the mid-1870s a very large group of Mennonites emigrated to Canada from the Bohemian section of Austria-Hungary to escape religious prosecution. They were pacifists in a war-like time and place. The largest portion of this group settled in Canada's new "West," the provinces of Alberta and Saskatchewan. As the railroads came into the area, the group prospered from the easier marketing of its wheat, oats, and rye. As is usual in a peaceful and prosperous place, the enclave multiplied and the area was soon overcrowded. As a result there was pressure for groups to split off from the "Mother Group" and emigrate once more.

Some of the splinter groups went to other places in Canada, but most went to newly-opened agricultural areas in the United States. Though geographically distant from one another, these groups maintained communication as well as a mutual sense of brotherhood through their religion.

Athena remarked at one point that the universal problem of close-knit enclaves is the knowledge among members that any other member is, in all probability, a blood relation. In such clans, lines of relationship become so tangled and lost in the mists of time that no one can follow them; nonetheless all are aware of their existence.

In 1915, when Canada was deeply involved in the European war, serious friction emerged within the country's generally intensely pacifist Mennonite community. Some of the young men enlisted and went off to war but a sizable group of Mennonites—largely young, unmarried service-age men, but a number of elders and couples with large families as well, pulled up stakes and, with the financial backing of the larger community, emigrated to Mexico. Thereby hangs Athena's tale.

The various Mennonite communities of North America and, especially, the mother community in Canada, remained in contact with their religious brethren in Mexico for some seventy years, ever since the time of World War I. For quite some years they also aided the Mexican Mennonite community financially but, in more recent years, suspicion began to grow that the southern kin were backsliding. Thus, after extensive planning, and with financial backing from both Canadian and U.S. Mennonites, Athena's and "my" rescue mission was put into action.

Lengthy correspondence was conducted between the various American groups and their kin in Mexico as well as between the Canadian and United States governments and the Mexican authorities.

Athena was chosen to be the Mennonite Saint Francis of Assisi for several reasons. First were her obvious physical attributes; second, the fact that she had attended, at least part-time, a college-in Moose Jaw; and third, her experience as a driver (having for some two years worked as a semi-driver on the Winnipeg-Edmonton-Calgary run). As additional preparation for her safari, Athena had also undertaken an assiduous study-by-tape of Spanish for speaking and listening comprehension. While I feared that she would be disappointed, I did not mention this to her.

Having mentioned the word "Mennonite," I will diverge here, yet again—as my wife and children will know, is my wont—to tell you of a previous encounter with a Mennonite, which marked only the second time in my life that I hitched a ride with an animal drawn vehicle. (The first was in Spain in 1944, but was undertaken by necessity, under the pressure of war and arranged for me by the French Underground or the British Intelligence, I don't know which, but that is another tale for another time.)

This was in Central Canada, some 400-500 miles west of Winnipeg. I was standing by the road, the main East-West Trans-Canadian Highway. There was damned little traffic, when down the road came an Amish vehicle: two nice horses and a four-wheeled rig with steel rimmed wheels. I stuck up my trusty thumb, more or less from habit, and the pilot of the four wheeled schooner pulled up and asked, "Dost thou have troubles? Please join us." "Us" consisted of an elderly Amish gentleman and three granddaughters, in the ten-to-fourteen year old range. For lack of anything better to do, I joined this happy crew and clip-clopped for an hour or so.

When my black-hatted, white-whiskered guardian angel said we would soon leave the road, he then asked, "Dost thou thirst or hunger?" Looking at the setting sun and aware that the next town was some 100 miles beyond the horizon, I said, "I dost." And thus said my patriarch, "Shalt thou be our guest for the night?" I, after thinking it over for all of ten seconds, said I shalt. So off we went, across about a mile and a half of this endless flat landscape, to the Amish homestead, a cluster of five or six houses and several rather large barns for their thirty or forty draft and driving horses.

I soon learned that the community's main cash crop is oats—Tis too far north for wheat — and that their oats are all raised in the old fashioned way: horse plowing, planting, cutting with binder, and so on, just as I remember doing when I was young. The crop is now all in the shock, some 2000 acres and threshing begins next week. They have a guaranteed buyer for their crop at fifty dollars per ton more than the market quote. Due to its superior quality, it all goes to Quaker Oats Company in St. Louis and is processed for "human consumption." They also have vast vegetable gardens; a fair sized herd of cattle (all for their own use for meat, milk, and other by products); chickens for eggs and meat; and a gaggle of geese for meat and feathers. The enclave seems to have one communal root cellar, partly underground and frost proof, a dugout type building measuring probably fifteen by sixty feet, wherein several families keep endless rows of home canned food, vegetables, meat, juices, bins of fresh vegetables, dozens of cured "deep-smoked" hams and some "corned beef" (both salted and smoked).

At any rate, mein host, Jonas Hoff-something-or-other, summoned his hausfrau, a fairly aged white-haired lady, dressed in black attire from shoes to bonnet, who spoke only German. Jonas spoke some English but he, too, preferred the Mother Tongue. The mid-aged group, those between thirty and fifty-five, spoke good English to me; a mixture of the two languages to each other; and German to their elders. The group under thirty spoke English to each other and to the kids. The kids spoke English most of the time, but German to "Grandpapa" and "Grandmama." (I got the impression that they were not at ease with the language.)

The meal to which I was summoned was completely homegrown: a whole loin of pork — slightly smoked — and every kind of vegetable that can be grown in this area, including some kind of a hot potato dish with vinegar. All very simple but excellent, and washed down with hot tea and fresh milk that waas no more than twenty minutes from the cow. The meal was consumed with great gusto and speed and then, as if by magic, the women, children, and dirty dishes disappeared, leaving us men — Jonas, two of Jonas' sons, two sons-in-law, and myself – –with six very large glasses of beet wine (which was not particularly good, but was strong and free). These people regard beer and wine as a regular part of their diet but do not over indulge.

Soon it was bedtime and all seemed to retire at once. I was ushered to a small but immaculate room in which was a bed with a soft mattress and a coverlet of goose down that was about three inches thick but had a total weight of probably less than two pounds. It was so warm one could have slept on a polar ice cap in comfort.

In the morning a rooster woke me with his crowing. My sleep disturbed, I thought, tis well he crows now, as ere fall he will be in the pot or the can. Went to the "rest room," four identical outdoor privies, one for each family apparently, which was as clean as the kitchen. Couldn't help but wonder about them being two-holers but suppose this has always been the design.

Heard a summons from the matriarch: "Guten morgan. Kom!" or something like that. I joined Jonas and Frau for breakfast, a splendid repast of large fluffy pancakes, great slabs of home-cured ham, home-churned butter, and tea—one and all delicious, filling, and free.

Had some conversation in broken English with Jonas. He seemed to be reluctant to try his English with the Grand Frau present. All of a sudden he rose, thanked me—At least I think he did—and then pointed towards the lane where a stripling of twelve to fourteen years waited. Jonas and Frau both pressed my hand warmly and I theirs. Jonas said, "You go now."

I went and joined the stripling and we clip-clopped back to the main highway. The lad said not a word, being too shy, I think, to expose his ignorance of the "outside." The lad deposited me on the main highway, gave a shy wave, and went back down the lane. While I was headed somewhere west, he was going back to the only place he would probably ever know. Which of our ways is the best, I know not nor will ever know but I do have a most fond memory of my sojourn among that most gentle and generous people. And while their ways are theirs and mine are mine, I will forever wonder if "progress" might not in truth be regression.

So, it was with that recoilection, I placed a bet with myself on Athena's origins. I guessed that she was probably related, one way or another, to that family I had met so many years before. My thoughts of them gave me a certain optimism about the road ahead.

My optimisn proved not to be displaced for the trip with Athena from Kansas to Mexico did, indeed, prove to be pleasant and congenial.

On our first day of travel together we ended the day at a Mennonite enclave in Texas where Athena stopped to speak to some brethren with whom she had been in correspondence. These people, wheat and vegetable farmers most of them, were fairly recent emigrants to Texas, and Athena had a vague memory of some of them from childhood.

We were invited to spend the night at the home of her newly-found kinfolk—welcome words, indeed, to the ears of a weary wayfarer traveling on limited funds.

After a plain but substantial meal that night, I was shown to a rather sparse but comfortable bedroom by a youngish man who said to me with an accent completely foreign to my ears, "We arise early. Sleep if you wish and good night."

In the morning I was awakened by a veritable chorus of crowing cocks. Though early, I thought I would arise and explore the area but my foray was cut short, lasting for only a few minutes, before I heard Athena's godly voice calling to me from an adjoining house: "Our breakfast is on, Little Father."

It seems that several of the young men in the community work on ranches a number of miles away and had to be off. That was the explanation for our breakfast being served at 6:30 A.M.

After breakfast I thanked my generous hosts and hostesses— As there were about a half dozen adults around the place and I didn't know who was in charge, I thanked them all!—and then went out to the van to wait for Athena, who arrived shortly thereafter bearing a large hamper of non-perishable food. Enough, it seemed to me, for a full-scale invasion of Mexico.

With our bellies and our hamper full we made our way south through Texas, Texas, and more Texas. We didn't push hard, however, and stopped at several places of historical and scenic interest, each time partaking of some of the succulent plunder in our hamper. (Greek goddesses seem to have both a healthy curiosity and appetite, but then we immortals can do pretty much as we damned well please!)

We took turns driving that day and at sundown found ourselves northwest of San Antonio. As the sun was setting we pulled into a woebegone little park in a rather woebegone looking town. Standing across the street from the park were a couple of men, small-town bank-clerk types by the look of them, and Athena exited the van to have a word with them. As she strode towards them in her most regal manner, I could see the expression on their faces change first to amazement, then to awe, and then to admiration.

Athena asked the men if it would be okay to stay the night in the park. The two men leaned back and gazed up at this godly apparition and more or less stammered, "Sure, fine, okay."

On returning to the van Athena and I made up our beds for the night, hers in the cab and mine in the back. After moving around numerous boxes, bags and bales, I managed to excavate a cavity of sufficient size in which to wedge this powerful frame and, frankly speaking, with a folded blanket for my mattress and a pair of shoes for a pillow, it proved to be not bad at all—but then that must be what a young Trappist feels on his first night in his monkery.

I slept fairly well and awoke to the sound of Athena rummaging around for something in the van. After finding whatever she was looking for, she then left the chariot. Following her lead, I too dismounted, then put on my shoes, combed my hair, and was ready to face another day. In the meantime my doughty goddess had already rustled up some dry wood, started a fire in a rusty park grill, and was preparing some very strong-smelling coffee in one pot and stewing some very hard but tasty sausages in another. That plus some home-made rye bread smeared with great gobs of peach jam made for a most substantial breakfast, more than I would ordinarily eat in a week, but one of the rules of the road is to eat when you can, especially if it's free.

Thus fortified, we returned to our trusty Canadian steed and headed south, our planned destination for the day being a Mennonite settlement located several miles up the Rio Grande from Brownsville, Texas. That was also to be the launch site for our invasion of Mexico.

Travel we did, merrily rolling our way, but stopping to rest at various points of interest and consume more goodies. During the course of the day I purchased several cans of cold soda, the first time my hands had been in my own pockets since leaving Jake's Innery in Nebraska.

With Athena's map work and navigation, we arrived at our destination smack on the temporal head of 2:00 P.M. which was about two hours earlier than we had actually expected to arrive.

The Mennonite community in which I found myself had been established fifty or sixty years previously but was still remarkably close-knit, and prosperous as well, due to its successful citrus operation, income from which was supplemented by additional profit from the sale of vegetables and lettuce.

We immortals were both expected and welcomed and while Athena got acquainted with her long lost kinfolk, I was left to wander about the grapefruit groves where I fell into conversation with any victim I could corner.

In general the people were a taciturn lot, still very insular, and speaking in very formal English but with an accent of mixed sounds: Canadian, German, Austrian and, last but not least, Spanish—not surprising, of course, since Mexico is in sight of the town, just across the Rio Grande, which, at that particular geographical point, was hardly worthy of the name "river," the water having for a thousand miles already been diverted for irrigation projects. (I don't know where the derogatory term "wet back" comes from, but in that place "damp feet" would have been the more apt epithet .)

After returning to the main house I was fed the usual large but simple meal but then quite abruptly shown to my quarters, which was a large and well-appointed room with a semi-private bath attached. As there was no shower I shaved and bathed in the tub, then went to bed. The pictures and knickknacks in the room clearly showed that a pair of teenage daughters had been evicted for my benefit, but I was not about to worry about that. It was a nice room and I was able to get a good sleep.

At an early hour in the morning I was awakened by a discreet knocking sound emanating from near the top of the bedroom door and the lilting voice of the Greek goddess singing, "Breakfast is ready if you are." I was soon ready and after breakfast we took off for the city of Brownsville on the Mexican border. I gathered from Athena that she had spent most of the night speaking with her formerly unknown kinfolk but, once again, this proves we immortals need very little sleep at all.

Arriving in Brownsville, we prepared to mount our final attack. First, Athena took our trusty van to a filling station for an oil change, a minor check-up, and gas. (Purchasing the gas there was a mistake as it was just half the price across the border.) Then, on advice of the previous night's kinfolk, she went to a bank and changed her U.S. and Canadian money into pesos. Almost all her funds were in Canadian hundred-dollar travelers checks which, she had been warned, would be difficult to exchange anywhere except at banks in the larger cities.

I too exchanged some money, about one third of my still largely intact funds, then set off to face our first hurdle: the customs officers at the border. Athena, with her canned Spanish, showed great confidence, but I was somewhat concerned about the large number of bales, bundles, and other items of cargo in her van. Fortunately, all the items were meticulously labeled in both English and Spanish and Athena had with her a sheaf of documents from the Mexican minister of something or other and the Canadian government as well, quite enough to awe any middle-level bureaucrat, to say nothing of the humble guardians of the empire with whom we were dealing. Quite impressed, the customs officers proceeded to sign and stamp everything in sight, including my left elbow on which an impressive stamp was laid.

Our personal luggage was a different kettle of fish. I, with just one small bag, encountered no difficulty but Athena, as befitting an extra-large goddess, was carrying two extra-large and extra-ornate caribou skin suitcases. It was the first real test of her Spanish which, given the disapproving look on our worthy functionaries' faces, did not go terribly well. Athena, assumed that it was their inability to understand her perfect Spanish that was creating the problem, one that I thought I might be able to clear up through my fluency in universal sign language. A handshake, I thought, might do, and it did.

As any speaker of universal sign language knows, there are numerous kinds of handshakes: the warm shake of welcome, the sad shake of parting, the polite shake of introduction, and so on. In this instance, however, I assumed that an "effective shake" might be in order and so, unbeknownst to Athena, for she would have disapproved, I tucked a few peso bills in my good right hand and introduced myself to one of the functionaries. Athena by this time was becoming rather pouty, thinking there no good reason in the world for those yokels not to understand her fluent Spanish.

The officer I spoke with turned out to be a pleasant young man who was semi-fluent in English. After we had shaken hands he cheerfully drew duplicate pictures for us of all pertinent road signs in both English and Spanish. All in all, he was very helpful, but then I was, too.

After finally crosing the border, we proceeded onward. We stopped for gas once and made several brief stops to observe the rather primitive agricultural methods that were being used in a land far more mountainous than I had expected. We also stopped at a roadside stand for a mysterious but satisfying meal.

The two-lane road that took us through the mountains was fairly good and sundown found us a little southeast of the large city of Monterey. As neither of us cared to drive at night, we looked for and found a place to bivouac—an empty lot beside a government-run filling station.

Athena tried out her canned Spanish again and this time seemed to be able to communicate fairly well for which she was childishly proud.

We had a light meal at a roadside stand twenty or thirty feet from our van and then went to bed, Athena to the cab and I to my Trappist cell.

I slept well and awoke to the call of the ubiquitous cock. (I can't imagine that there would be any market for alarm clocks south of Kansas!) While Athena tidied up her living quarters and studied the maps and documents in her briefcase, I sauntered over to the food stand and had a glass, or rather a cup, of excellent fruit juice. There, I also fell into conversation with an elderly gentleman by the name of José who, as it turned out, had worked in Chicago and Milwaukee for some twenty-three years and spoke English fairly well. When learning that my home was in Wisconsin, he immediately queried me about the Green Bay Packers and Milwaukee Brewers.

José had managed to save a good bit of money when living in the States and now received a monthly Social Security check from the U.S. Government as well. He said, quite simply and with no show of braggadocio, "It makes me rich there. Now I own my own home and little farm." Then, with obvious pride, he added, "My son graduates from the University of Illinois at Christmas time."

I didn't think to ask José whether he was a U.S. citizen but that was irrelevant to our conversation. He was a cordial fellow and I would have liked to spend more time with him, but then Athena came over, ordered some juice and what looked to be a flat corn pancake and, after chatting with my new acquaintance, said to me, "Well, Little Father, I suppose we'd better go."

José shook my hand and after glancing with awe at Athena, said to me in parting, "Congratulations on your daughter's grande figure," or something like that.

Our tentative schedule for the day was to travel via what looked on the map to be fairly good roads to a "lost" Mennonite settlement somewhere to the southwest of the city of Agua Calienté. This settlement, the exact whereabouts of which were unknown, was an offshoot not of the Canadian Mother Community but of a different migration of Mennonites, this one from the Eastern United States. As a result, there had been scant communication between the Mother Community and this particular settlement.

Our southerly journey that day took us through an arid, mountainous region with a surprisingly large number of intensive small farming operations.

We stopped once for gas and a snack and once just to snack and observe the work at an extremely primitive adobe block manufactory. In that area it seems the rainfall was sufficient enough to greatly diminish the life expectancy of adobe and for that reason there was a continuous demand for blocks. Most of the houses looked to be in an on-going state of repair or replacement.

Children, chickens, and goats were kings of the road in that area and their continual presence was enough to keep any driver alert. I did most of the driving, as Athena was busy studying maps and written directions. Frankly, I *allowed* her to think she was doing the navigating but such a skill is not in fact a forte of the immortals.

Around mid-day we approached Agua Calienté. Our map, an official Mexican government tourism map, showed an elaborate new four-lane road passing around the city, but because we could find no evidence of it I pulled into a large government-run filling station in search of information.

Athena first tried communicating with an attendant in Spanish but with unsatisfactory results. (She was constantly being shocked at how little Spanish these natives knew!) But then I found, among the many employees, a couple of young fellows who spoke a fair brand of broken English which they had picked up as high school students in Arizona and California where their parents had worked in the fields, groves, and vineyards of those two states. One of the two had also spent two of his young adult years doing the same thing and, possessing some kind of a card— a green card, I assume — was able to return to the States to work if he so wished.

In a foreign culture it is always best to establish a certain rapport with a person or people before one starts asking questions; it helps avoid misunderstandings. This having been done, I got out Athena's map and showed them the bypass we were seeking. Both young men laughed and extended their hands, palms up, and said, "Mañana." They then explained that the well-marked by-pass "might" be started in a few years. It seems the tourism and road-building authorities in Mexico are completely out of synch.

As there was nothing else for us to do but to charge through the center of the city, charge is what we did, this time with Athena driving and I in the navigator's seat. The city was much larger than either of us had expected, with upwards of one million inhabitants, and not "laid out" like any city we knew. Like Topsy, it seems, the place just grew.

My navigational fix was a large mountain peak far to the south; I assumed that if we kept going in that direction we would eventually emerge on the southern side of the city near the main road to Mexico City. (*Hitchhiker's note: the closer to the equator one travels, the less help the sun will be as it is almost directly overhead and casts few useable shadows.*) In the end, the mountain served very well. There was, of course, the remote chance that the peak would move on us, but that was a chance we had to take. (Just consider poor old Christopher Columbus who had two continents jump in his way, yet he never knew what had happened to him and didn't even know where he had been when he returned, but his name still be blessed!)

At any rate, in due time we arrived at the southern extremities of the city and within a mile or so of our hoped for landfall, the main road to Mexico City. We had several adventures and misadventures en route, but on the whole, it went fairly well. Our misadventures were due to the way the city was "laid out." You'd have a half mile of a good north-south street which would then end with the choice of having to turn right or left. After meandering through three or four blocks of narrow alley-type trail—Presto!—you'd find another section of well-built and heavily-traveled north-south street. I felt it was a triumph of driving and navigation skills to emerge where we did.

The "adventure" was the traffic. The streets or whatever they are called in this city serve as both the playground and daytime home for hordes of happy children — and a lot of not-so-happy goats and chickens, all of whom seem to have a burning desire to get to the other side of the street, right now! And that is what they constantly did.

Vehicular traffic was also heavy, with all types of semi-trucks, decrepit pick-ups, cars of every vintage, horse and donkey carts and wagons, and an occasional bullock cart as well. It was a bit frightening at first, at least for Athena, but after a while became almost enjoyable.

Once we were back on the main road we headed towards Athena's ultimate objective, with a tentative stop scheduled fifty or sixty miles down to the road to check on one of the lost tribes of the Mennonites. I personally doubted that we would find anything. For one thing, there had been little communication between this community and Athena's Canadian enclave and, more significantly, after three generations as a tiny minority in a foreign land, I suspected that the tribe had been completely absorbed into the larger culture. The history of both Latin and Oriental civilizations provide ample evidence for my assumption but I hesitated to mention such suspicions to my Greek Goddess.

We arrived in the general vicinity of the lost colony and, having lost much of our confidence in tourist maps, decided to seek information from the local inhabitants. Athena tried her Spanish on some of the older citizens but with no luck. I found a middle-aged man who had worked as a migrant laborer in the United States for several years and who spoke fair English, but all he could tell me was that some years ago there had been a couple of older men in the area who spoke to each other in either German or English but they were now dead. As that seemed to be that, and as Athena hoped to reach her ultimate destination the next day, we decided to drive on until evening and bivouac again.

Nighttime found us in a small city about two hundred miles from Mexico City. There we parked our bed-on-wheels in the parking lot of a minor-league bullfight arena which, fortunately for us, was not in use at the time. (In fact, within Mexico's bull-fighting constellation, that arena was probably a training ground where hopeful young toreadors learned the fine art of slaying hopeless young bulls, laboring in hopes of being called up to the major leagues where they would slay bigger bulls in front of bigger crowds for bigger money.)

We ate a meal at one of the many open-air restaurants near the arena—It's remarkable how many Mexican restaurants are to be found in this land!—and thereafter retired to our respective cells.

Morning brought with it the crowing of the ever-present cocks, and my how those cocks do crow! After performing such ablutions as were possible, we then set off on our last lap together, making our way across miles of high plain, occasionally fringed with higher mountains. The generally bare landscape was dotted with islands of intensely-farmed land—mostly beans and peppers—which I was to learn bore two crops per year. There was a bit of livestock, including yoked cattle for farm work.

On and on we went until about 2:00 P.M. when we finally arrived at Athena's Mecca. We found the place with no trouble but within minutes I surmised that Athena was in for disappointment. It was obvious that all but the oldest of the people

47

were thoroughly Mexicanized, both culturally and ethnically.

We were extended a hearty welcome but I felt an awkwardness in the air and thought it best that I bid farewell to my traveling companion. (I was already thinking of my return trip and wondering whether to travel back north via the coastal route or to return on the road that had brought us to this place.) When I communicated my wishes to Athena, she protested; she had already spoken to her kinfolk about me staying the night. Nonetheless, I insisted that I must go.

After some talk with Athena's kinfolk, a linguistic trial in itself as these formerly sturdy Austrian-Canadians had almost completely converted to Mexican culture, one woman informed me that her nephew, Gottlieb, owned a truck line and hauled fruit to Vera Cruz. Maybe she could arrange a ride with him, she posed, which sounded good to me. Another woman said that her sister-in-law Ita lived in the city and "let" rooms. The upshot of this conclave was that Athena and two of her kin escorted me to Ita's, stopping briefly along the way at the headquarters of the aforementioned "truck line" to see about the possibility of me getting a ride to the coast.

With little trouble, we located nephew Gottlieb and received from him an effusive welcome due to the fact that one of my escorts was an in-law of his, another was one of his favorite cousins, and Athena was a person he had long looked forward to meeting.

It turned out that "Gott," as he was called, was going to Vera Cruz and that I was welcome to come along for the ride. Arrangements were made for Gott to pick me up at Ita's two days hence.

When leaving I was gratified to hear Gott say in an aside to one of my guardian angels, "*Gringo bueno*," or something like that—an expression of approval, I guessed.

48

At Ita's, my three guardian angels quickly arranged two night's lodging for me at a very modest price. I held out what peso notes I had and the four of them picked them over, returning to me what I felt to be a good percentage of the original sum.

Now came the time to part with my Greek Goddess. After some thousands of miles we had developed a true rapport and a father-daughter kind of affection. Our parting was abrupt but warm. "Good bye, Little Father," she said, then leaned over and gave me an affectionate kiss on the top of my head and was gone. She was a lovely person of impressive proportions and I shall always think of her in her rightful milieu—standing regally in her own temple in Athens or possibly, in her spare time, atop the Statue of Liberty pedestal in New York's harbor.

As I have already described my first night in Mexico City, we shall skip to the second day of my brief tour of one of the world's largest cities.... That morning I was awakened early by the cock's crow. My scrawny alarm clock, standing on the window sill, was not to be denied, so I arose, washed up as best I could with the limited facilities, changed into the clean clothes I had been hoarding, and sallied forth to meld myself into the teeming masses.

I walked down to what appeared to be a main thoroughfare, already crowded at that early hour with humanity and chickens and all in one hell of a hurry to get from one place to another. Soon thereafter push-cart cafes began to appear and I partook of a breakfast of excellent crushed fruit and some kind of corn pancake cooked on tiny butane griddles inside the vendor's cart. They were hotter than the devil on the outside and ten times as hot on the inside, stuffed as they were with meat and explosive peppers.

49

I won't try to describe the city as that would be presumptuous after having spent only one day there but I did manage to see a good bit of the place in the limited time at my disposal. I spent a fair share of the day just watching people which is, I find, a much better pastime than studying statues or museums if one wants to capture the feeling of a large city in a strange land.

Two of the places I visited deserve mention. The first was a vast market (one of the few I visited that day), part of which was roofed, part of which was open-air, and containing thousands of traders' stalls, a veritable maze of narrow alleys with the vendors selling anything that was edible and, I fear, much that was not edible as well.

Milling about were thousands of shoppers, mostly women, purchasing small quantities of goods, probably no more than two or three days worth of household supplies. There was remarkably little haggling, possibly because there were so many stalls selling the same produce.

I came across one lady operating a stall who spoke rather good English and was kind enough, in the time permitted, to explain a little of the history of that vast food mart. She explained that the market dated back to the days of Cortez.

I just mentioned that anything and everything was sold there, but the beans, ye gods, the beans! There were beans of every size, shape and color and in such quantities as would stagger the imagination.

The peppers too were yet another "ye-gods," with there, again, being every size and shape and color imaginable in vast quantities. I don't know this for a fact, but I suspect that each vendor tries to sell peppers that are hotter than those of her neighbor. A non-scientific idea of mine is that if all the peppers were piled together and their heat released simultaneously, it would make an atomic bomb seem like a firecracker.

There were also meat stalls, some for poultry, either alive or partially dressed. There was a vast number of chickens and a somewhat lesser number of ducks, geese, and a large-winged beast resembling a turkey. There were also meat stalls featuring freshly butchered cattle, goats, and sheep. A customer would point out the cut of meat and size he wanted; the butcher would expertly detach the requested piece, wrap the meat in used newspaper, and send the customer on his way.

The fish section was relatively small due to the fact that supplies of fish for that working-class market come from the distant Gulf of Mexico and the transportation system is spotty at best. On the day I visited, the supply was meager and what was being sold had seen much better days. The eyes of the fish were sunken, their faces sad-looking, and they had a decided odor.

I'm sure I could have spent a week in that market and still not seen all that there was worth seeing, especially the people.

The other memorable site for me was Mexico City's main cathedral, located about a mile from the market. The place was immense and some parts of it very old. Construction of this "Mother Church" for Latin America began in the early 1600s, but numerous structural additions resulting from the area's recurrent earthquakes have made the place very confusing.

The two most impressive things about the site were the church's wooden doors and the throngs of happy people milling about. The doors are massive things, standing about thirty feet high and made from solid hand-hewn planks of at least four inches thick and ten to twenty inches wide. Where they originated, I don't know but I would guess from several hundred miles away at least.

51

No large trees grow or have ever grown at such a high altitude as Mexico City's.

The doors are fitted together with wooden dowels and the hinges—four absolutely massive ones on each door—are of hand-wrought iron. The entire assembly is probably three centuries old yet just as tight as when it was installed. However, I don't think that they have swung shut in a century or more.

Unfortunately I had no chance to strike up a conversation with any of the people there, but the plaza in front of the church. — its broad steps, and, to some extent, its vast interior — — appeared to be a place for family get-togethers, picnics, and occasional prayer. From time to time a terrified rooster would charge in with a laughing boy in hot pursuit. I saw several dark-robed priests about the place acting as both janitors or confessors. But as the sun was sinking in the west (as it usually does), it was time to hike myself back to Ita's room.

Having set up my landmarks for triangulation the night before, I had little trouble finding Ita's place and arrived "home" just as the sun was setting and the tumult and shouting from the courtyard was dying down. As it was time for bed, to bed I went.

I was awakened at dawn the next morning by my raucous cock crowing on the window sill. This time, to make his message even more explicit, he had recruited two of his brethren and together they convinced me to rise. After dressing, I chased those damned alarm clocks from my chamber, did what little packing was necessary, and was ready to meet the day and also Gottlieb, my ride to the Gulf of Mexico.

As it was only about 7:00 A.M. and I didn't expect Gottlieb and his truck till mid-morning, I thought I'd amble over a couple of blocks to the street where the push-cart cafes had been the day before and have a spot of breakfast but I was stopped by the sound of Ita calling cheerily, "*Buenos dias, gringo*," or something like that. Henceforth, Ita came to me bearing a wicker tray with my breakfast. (I gathered that she had done the same the day before but I had already left.)

Breakfast consisted of a small cup of beastly strong coffee, a very small but tasty citrus fruit and a deep-fried cake of some sort consisting of corn meal, diced beef, and the inevitable chilie pepper. Tasty it was, but a little to hot for my taste.

I sat on the wicker divan with Ita on the other end. As before, we tried to talk in sign language but that was a particularly difficult exercise for me as my hands were occupied and my mouth was full. Nevertheless, we had a jolly talk and when I finished eating, Ita gathered up her tray, looked at me quizzically, and said, "Mañana?" To which I shook my head and answered, "Gottlieb." She smiled and said, "Si," obviously having forgotten our arrangements. She then said something else—"Goodbye," I presume—and waddled regally away.

I thought it best to go out to the street and wait for Gott there. The single-lane street was very narrow with the houses on both sides abutting one another, giving the street the appearance of a walled lane. Each of the houses had a wide arched doorway opening onto an inner courtyard, something that seemed to be a very sensible and cozy arrangement in such a congested area.

I had been on the street about an hour when my ridee, Gottlieb, and his "truck line" arrived. (Gott's "truck line" consisted of one venerable flatbed truck and Gott himself.) The truck, a GMC, was a survivor of many years and numerous battles.

Within an hour of our departure it became evident that Gott

and I were extremely compatible. He was an exceptionally jolly fellow and spoke a fair grade of broken English. I learned that he was a third-generation descendent of one of the original Mennonite immigrants. He had either one-quarter or one-eighth Norse blood but that was barely detectable. His three children of course have but one half of that fraction. As to his incongruous name, it seems that the Austrian-Canadian immigrants soon adopted the Latin custom of incorporating the mother's maiden name in some sequence; hence, my jolly companion's name was "Gottlieb Jesus R'Chavez." But anyone can call themselves what they damned well please. It's the person that counts, and Gott was a jewel.

When Gott picked me up that morning in Mexico City his truck was about half full of cactus fruit packed in wooden boxes. By the time we arrived in Vera Cruz he hoped to have a full load and was planning on filling the rest of his truck with purchases at several small markets along the way. As a result, our speed of travel on the approximately two-hundred mile trip was very slow. Fortunately, the trip was very scenic.

The route we followed was almost exactly the reverse of the one made by Cortez and, about three hundred years later, by U.S. Army troops under the leadership of General Winfield Scott. I had read considerably of these two plunderous expeditions and, fortunately for me, Gott was well versed in the history, geography, and folklore of this part of Mexico. (Such native wisdom and understanding would of course be *verboten* subjects in U.S. schools for not having been set down as gospel by some tenured egghead who knew nothing of the facts of life.)

As I just mentioned we had to stop at several small market towns. After leisurely and good-naturedly haggling in each of these towns, Gott was able to acquire most of the volume he needed to complete his load but, as siesta was calling by the time this task was completed and as it was not for another thirty-six hours that Gott was due in Vera Cruz, he decided to rest a bit with some of his friends.

Not used to the civilized custom of sleeping in the afternoon, I found shelter under a thatched shed and did some writing. While sitting there, writing a little, dreaming a little, and admiring the mountain scenery, who should appear before my eyes but a lovely señorita. Unfortunately this apparition disappeared as quickly as it appeared but left behind was what I thought was a large glass of water – at least that is until I took a large swallow of it. A clear fluid, it was, but water it was not. For a moment I thought a rocket had been launched in my throat.

After making a reasonably dignified landing and checking for burned tonsils, I began a careful study of the innocent glass and its explosive contents. First I sniffed and then I sipped. The verdict was alcohol, but having been challenged, I resolved to meet the challenge and, with one sip at a time, I managed to vanquish that fiery concoction.

At the height of my battle with the glass, Gott and a friend of his arrived. Gott introduced the man, the local fruit broker it seems, who had helped Gott round up enough exotic fruit to complete our load. A good thing, too, for we were close to the edge of cactus country and from that point onward we would make our descent towards the coast with the beautiful mountain scenery quickly changing from semi-arid to lush tropical vegetation.

Gott asked me how I liked my drink. Through fiery tears, I assured them that it was excellent, if perhaps a wee bit weak. At this vainglorious remark, they both exploded in laughter. (I, too, felt in danger of exploding, but not with laughter.) They informed me that the enemy with whom I had wrestled was one hundred proof locally-distilled tequila which is usually cut with seventy-five percent water and citrus juice. My brave battle seemed to make me a full member of some secret fraternity.

Gott announced that his broker friend had asked us to stay the night at his hacienda. That sounded good to me—one of the cardinal rules of the road is to accept anything offered but to never ask for anything—and we swiftly mounted Gott's "truck line" and followed his friend to a hacienda a mile or two off the main road on the outskirts of a small village. There I was shown to my quarters, a pavilion or guest house standing a short distance from the main hacienda, which itself was a small but well-kept house.

My private castle, measuring approximately twelve by fourteen feet, was equipped with a comfortable cot, a small mirror, a small chest of drawers on which a large wash basin and two small towels had been placed. Outside, in the courtyard was a hand-operated water pump, where I also noticed busily scratching the ground a small flock of self-winding alarm cocks.

Gott and his friend invited me to dine with them that evening but I, as politely as possible, declined the offer, saying I was not in the least bit hungry. They both smiled knowingly and took off to load the rest of Gott's cargo. In spite of having my enemy surrounded I thought it unwise to provide it any form of reinforcements, especially in the shape of red-hot peppers. Nonetheless, as there were still two hours of daylight and the enemy within seemed to be subdued, I decided to tour the nearby village.

The village was small and most of its inhabitants seemed to be engaged in marginal farming activities though, given the time of the day it was, about the only activities one could see on the unpaved streets were children playing, goats doing whatever goats do, and the ubiquitous chickens doing whatever chickens do. I toured the entire town in an hour or so. There were a few small shops, all of them "manned" by women. There was also a modest central market with a dozen or so stalls and the inevitable open-air Mexican restaurant.

By this time my stomach felt secure in its victory and sent the message that a bit of food would be welcome. I answered the call and acquired at the restaurant a very tasty container of crushed fruit. Feeling more adventurous I then tried a couple of deep fried balls made of corn, bits of chopped meat, and hot peppers. Either the local peppers were not as potent as those of the city or I was developing an immunity, the food did not taste too hot. At any rate, as my stomach absorbed this tasty and filling nourishment, I felt that after having conquered the midday enemy, that ungodly slug of straight tequila, a bottle of warm Mexican beer might do.

When the sun began to sink on the western horizon and the light, as if controlled by a dimmer switch, began to turn to darkness, I returned to the hacienda to arrange my nest for the night. Soon after arriving "home," I was ready to bed down, as was my retinue of walking alarm clocks.

Early the next morning I awoke to a most horrid cacophony of crowing cocks. I then shaved and bathed as well as I could with water from the pump in the rooster pasture. I was about to walk over to the main house in search of Gott when there appeared at my cottage a charming young señorita bearing my breakfast on a tray. Too shy to attempt any conversation, she disappeared as silently as she had appeared.

Breakfast consisted of small cup of very strong coffee, two small but extremely sweet bananas, and a slice of toast covered with jam, which was more than sufficient for me. I was about to go in search of my goodly Gott again when he himself appeared, apparently ready to go.

Gott's truck line was fully loaded with well-built wooden boxes, each one holding about two hundred pounds of the exotic and expensive cactus fruit. I calculated that the truck contained about three tons of the fruit. The boxes had easily-removable board tops, thereby making inspection at the destination easier.

I suggested that I call on our host to thank him before we departed, but Gott advised me, "Better not bother him. He is not too well." He didn't look too spry himself. I suspected that these two old friends had spent a rather festive night together and were now suffering for it.

We then mounted our trusty GMC and set off to the east. Though we had only about sixty miles to go, the first forty were extremely mountainous. The road was well paved but generally quite narrow with occasional wide spots for passing.

Shortly after leaving our night stop we began to make our way through the most awesome mountain scenery, mostly downwards, descending about eight thousand feet to sea level in a distance of only about twenty miles as the crow flies. There were a few small hillside farms along the way and as we descended the vegetation changed toward the tropical due to the lower altitude and greater rainfall.

Gott, who was extremely cognizant of historical matters, pointed out a number of level spots that had been used by various invaders as staging areas for battles and other sites of long-forgotten skirmishes.

After our descent from the mountain we came to a semi-tropical coastal plain and then to the city of Vera Cruz itself, which was much larger and more confusing than I had expected. Trusty and jolly Gott, however, was thoroughly familiar with all the streets, jogs, and speed bumps and we soon arrived at the city's large harbor where we found the broker or shipping agent, a man by the name of Carlos with whom Gott did his business. After having done business together for a number of years, their relationship seemed to be one of absolute trust.

Carlos, who looked to be typically Latin in appearance, did his business with Gott in Spanish but, when turned to me, spoke in a most formal Oxford-sort of British English with a distinctive Danish or Norwegian accent. His apparel was unusual: a well-made wide-brimmed white hat, a slightly soiled but well-cut white linen suit, and polished, pointed shoes. With a small black cigar continually attached to his lips, he reminded me of pictures of Mark Twain.

Carlos informed Gott that the shipment of and payment for his cargo was all arranged and that he had a load of something for Carlos to take back with him on his return trip. And no inspection of Gott's cargo would be necessary either, due to Gott's fine reputation. This information tickled Gott pink, as it inflated both his profit and ego. As a result, his cargo could be transferred directly from the truck to a coastal freighter, meaning that he wouldn't have to pay any longshoremen for their help.

As it would be a couple of hours before the unloading and loading were completed, I suggested to Gott and Carlos that they be my guests for lunch, an offer they accepted readily. My unwonted generosity had two thoughts as parents: the first being a combination of the sincere friendship that had developed between Gott and myself; the second being my curiosity about Carlos, who seemed to be a most interesting character.

Carlos guided us to a fair-sized and partially open-air eatery on the waterfront. He appeared to be a familiar face and we were immediately shown to a small table overlooking the busy but odiferous polyglot waterfront.

I asked Gott to order for me. After consultation with Carlos, our order was transmitted to a rather nondescript waiter and, in no time at all, our meal was there. Each of us was served half of a scrawny chicken, cooked cavity-side up with an egg and an unknown vegetable inside and spiced with hot peppers and some kind of fresh herb that was unknown to me. We were also served some strange sort of bean as well as corn bread and strong coffee (locally grown, according to Carlos). All were tasty and filling.

On finishing our meal we still had an hour or so to spend before getting back to the port so I suggested that maybe a spot of wine was in order. After thinking over the suggestion for about five seconds Carlos called out something and instantaneously three liter-sized bottles appeared. The beverage was cold and tasty and, as we sipped it, I began to act on the more devious reason for my hospitality. Knowing from observation that Carlos was a respected figure in the harbor area, I thought he might be of some use for me in catching free transportation north, possibly a truck heading up the coastal road. I mentioned this in passing.

After a bit of thought, Carlos shook his head and in his clipped English said that the road was no bloody good and would take forever, but that I might consider going by sea. Carlos then beckoned to a prosperous fellow at a nearby table and ordered four more beers, on me. The gentleman joined us and he and Carlos conversed in Spanish. The upshot of their conversation was that

Carlos would help me to get work and passage on the ship that was to carry Gott's fruit to the United States.

The other man was an officer or partner in a shipping outfit consisting of two over-aged and under-powered coastal freighters, of which my future "yacht" was one. He gave Carlos the go-ahead to tell the ship's captain anything he pleased.

Before departing for the wharf I had to settle the dining tab, which I decided it would be best for Gott to handle. I handed him my rather thin billfold—Most of my U.S. dollars were locked away inside my bag in Gott's truck—and he took care of the chore, returning to me my modest hoard not badly depleted.

At the port Gott positioned his vehicle alongside my private yacht and our cargo of fruit was swung aboard by means of a rather primitive boom and winch. As this was being done, Carlos and I boarded the royal tub to verify the various bills of lading with the captain and to talk to him about my presence on board.

The captain, a most mysterious looking character, was dressed in odd bits and pieces of nautical garb, but sported a very imposing cap with a large badge on it indicating that he was the captain and you'd damned well better believe it.

The negotiation of my passage from Treasure Island to the States was negotiated in three languages. Having been assured by Gott that I was a world famous chef (currently on the run from a South American dictator), I was signed on by the captain, or John Silver as I now regarded him, as chief cook at no pay and with the rather meaningful remark that his cabin was a couple bottles short of tequila.

I then left the yacht to fetch my modest baggage from Gott's truck and say *adios* to that kind, witty, and well-informed man. We both sincerely felt the sadness of parting. I then went to a grog shop across the way to replenish the Captain's supply, after which I reported to the deck for duty. John Silver accepted the initiation fee without comment, pointed to a couple of cots and a couple of hammocks and said, "Take your choice." He then showed me my tiny galley. "The damned crew will be too drunk tonight to eat," he commented. "But we'll sail in the morning." He also searched my handbag, apparently afraid that I might be carrying contraband. (What money I had left, I had, on Gotlieb's advice, secreted in the lining of a wind-breaker.) The captain then disappeared.

We cast off at dawn with our tons of cargo, mostly cactus fruit, heading towards Lake Charles, Louisiana, with an e.t.a. of four days or so. *"Mañana,"* is what I thought.

I performed my cookly duties—making strong coffee and scrambling some not too fresh eggs that I laced with diced red peppers, making them so blasted hot that if you had dropped them they would have burnt a hole in the deck. Surprisingly, the crew didn't growl too much and the captain even passed out a large bottle of warm, strong beer for dessert. Thereafter, most of the meals consisted of fried bananas and ample helpings of shrimp boiled in beer. (I never did manage to find where John Silver secreted the suds away.)

Each man was responsible for catching his own shrimp, trawling the water beside or behind our diesel powered tub with nets. The captain and I, having more free time than the rest of the crew, shared whatever shrimp we caught. Generally, there was more than enough to go around—all in all a very democratic crew of pirates.

The weather was perfect and the moon was full, enabling us

to arrive in Louisiana in three and a half day's time, a full day sooner than expected, a feat which earned the captain a bonus.

All in all it was a most enjoyable voyage with a very interesting crew of black guards. 'Twas now time to part and head home, but having promised the crew more tequila, I said that I would go to one of the numerous waterfront saloons and purchase some. The crew protested, primarily I believe because none of them trusted me to return—with good reason, as I had every intention of absconding as soon as I was out of sight—but also, because if I were to return to the ship with bottles, the captain would lock them up and drink them at his own leisure. As a compromise, one that was more or less forced on me, I then suggested that the men be my guests for a meal at one of the waterfront bistros patronized by the crews of undisciplined "coasters" such as our own. So off we went, my loyal crew hovering over their trusty cook as if they expected me to spread my wings and rise in flight.

Our meal I could only describe as some kind of South American concoction served from a large pot in middle of table and washed down with warm Mexican beer. The clientele and management of the eatery, a weird place if there ever was one, seemed to be conversant in every language known to man, except English.

Once sated, I parted from my motley crew and piratical captain with profuse declarations of affection.

The day being but half gone and the time of my expected arrival home growing shorter, I decided to put a few miles behind me before dark, and thereafter caught several medium-length rides, one with an elderly black gentleman who made his living fishing crabs. He gave me a thorough schooling in the intricacies of catching and marketing those noble beasts. While I'll probably never make use this wisdom, I might someday be able to impress someone in Wisconsin with my knowledge of crabbery.

I spent the night at a not-too-clean innery in a not-too-clean and fairly decrepit town.

The next day I headed north on one of the two roads out of town, making fairly good speed, catching one long ride with a prosperous rice farmer (whose lessons on rice culture served to further expand my field of expertise). Nighttime found me in a town in North Arkansas where I found lodging in a private home and spent only five dollars for a sparse but clean room and a breakfast of toast and coffee.

In the morning I left my previous night's bivouac and headed northeast, hoping to connect with a free ferry across the Mississippi north of Memphis and then proceed by way of Highway 57 northward through the length of Illinois to within a few miles of home.

My plan worked pretty well. My first ride was with a Baptist preacher who didn't preach much, but who did buy me breakfast, thank the Lord. The next ride brought me to within one half mile of the ferry across the Mississippi. I could have gone further with that ride but then I would have had to go through St. Louis. As a result, I was forced to swallow my pride and walk— actually walk—the half mile to the ferry.

On the ferry across the Mississippi I fell into conversation with a young couple who were going to Carbondale, Illinois, a town with which I was familiar, having hitchhiked through the place several times when on furlough in the Air Force some fifty-five or fifty-six years ago. They suggested that I could ride with them if I wished. Wish I did and in Carbondale I spent the night at a small hotel for railroad crews. The place was plain, cheap, and clean.

At the V.F.W Club that night I found, as is usual in a mid-sized town, the kind of local wit and wisdom most familiar to me. In this instance it was provided mostly by retired or "former" coal miners. I say "former" because while the area was once coal-mining country, there are no mines still open today. A few of the men I spoke with had served in World War II but most, I guessed, had never been more than one hundred miles from home and were, without exception, living on or below the "poverty line." Despite that, they seemed to have no desire to go anywhere; they didn't seem to feel there was any place else to go. All in all, it made me a little sad.

The next day, which turned out to be the last day of my trip, I left my lodgings in good time and, after a cup of coffee, was back to the thumb. My first ride was short, but entertaining. The driver was a social worker who seemed to regard anyone not riding in a chauffeured limo as a "potential case." (I guess if a case worker is to keep his or her job, they must have "cases.") I had the very devil of a time turning down the charming young lady's offer to join her in visiting one of her "cases" up the road whom she intended to have enrolled in every bureaucratic do-gooder pro-gram possible. (About this particular "case," she said, matter of factly, "I do hope he's sober enough to receive me.")

The next ride was a good one, on a refrigerated semi-truck, loaded with thirty thousand pounds of shrimp and crab and pi-loted by a Creole from North Dakota. We stopped for lunch and fuel at Rockford, Illinois, and he later dropped me off in Mauston. After two quick rides I was on my doorstep being welcomed home by wife and children.

After countless days away from home it was that night a most happy reunion as I laid my powerful frame to rest alongside my patient Penelope.

Rip, the Mystery Man

It is yet another Sunday afternoon in the Winter of 1996-97 and as the weather is bad, the football game on television not worth a damn, and Annie is sleeping, I'll jot down the remembrances of an interesting character I met a number of years ago during one of my sojourns out West.

The man's name was Rip, or so he said, and I met him in one of the country's last hobo jungles, in Laurel, Montana, where I happened to find myself a number of years ago.

As remembered from my youth — I had hopped many a ride on trains passing through the town — Laurel was a major switching and marshaling yard for freight trains; it was there that extra large locomotives were attached to West-bound trains. Thus, the rail yard and the town itself was a hive of activity. And on the edge of town were a large hobo jungle. (Of course, that was almost fifty years ago, in the days of the steam locomotive.)

On this trip so many years later, being that it was late afternoon when I arrived in Laurel, I decided to stop and spend the night and see how things had changed. I discovered they had changed greatly, primarily due to the adoption of diesel power. There was still quite a lot of activity in the yards and several hotels had been built as lodgings for train crews on layover and for salesmen traveling by train.

67

I found a very small, very plain, and very cheap room for myself and then sallied forth to explore the town. The switch yards were still quite large and busy, partly due to the preparations that took place there for trains on the mountain run and partly due to the fact that all switching activity from Billings some thirty miles to the East had been relocated there.

I couldn't find anybody with the time or inclination to talk so I returned to the street facing the yard on which my hotel was located. Discovering one of the town's landmarks, a saloon by the name of Sonny O'Dea's, I decided to delve into that particular landmark's history. So in I went.

As it turned out, the saloon and its proprietor could be the subject of a short book. But briefly, Sonny, the proprietor, who was then eighty-eight years old, had purchased the place in 1932. Prior to that he'd been a world light-weight boxing champion for ten years running and was called, according to the old handbills on the wall, "Sonny O'Dea: the Butte Battler."

After losing the title, he had returned from his travels to his home town of Butte and, following the end of Prohibition, drifted to Laurel, where he opened his saloon and has been a fixture of the town ever since.

When I entered the establishment, Sonny himself was behind the bar and, as he was not overly busy, we soon became engaged in an enjoyable conversation. He was a veritable walking encyclopedia of Western railroad history and also a compendium of the history of pugilism. He was a long-time friend of Jack Dempsey and several other well-known pugs.

The walls of his cozy little pub were literally covered with signed pictures of these worthies. Oddly, among them was a large picture of two beaming young Catholic nuns. Seeing my expression, Sonny proudly announced that these two young women were his daughters, born the last two years when he was champ. One was now a Mother Superior of a large house in Spokane; the other had spent her religious life among the Oglala in South Dakota. He fairly burst with pride when telling about them.

As Sonny now had a few customers on whom he had to attend, I decided to go, but before doing so I asked about the hobo jungle that I remembered. He said that it was still there, but very few bums came through anymore. I told Sonny I was going to walk to the site and look around. As I was leaving he called, "Drop in tonight and have one on me."

I walked down to the jungle and found that Sonny was right. There were but a few old derelicts leftover from days of yore. However, there was one who looked more promising. He looked cleaner and somewhat younger and was sitting in a discarded car seat reading a book. He seemed to have his own little shack, made with a wooden frame and covered with steel corrugated roofing. Inside I could see a camp cot and some pots and pans.

I said hello and, trying to be circumspect and not pushy, remarked that I was looking around to bring back memories of being here some fifty years before. That seemed to break the ice and he moved over and said, "Care to join me in the back seat of my Cadillac?"

Our conversation was tentative at first but soon warmed up. I told him my name and he said his name was Rip. That was it for a time. Then I mentioned again how things had changed since the 1930s and he replied, "It's changed a hell of a lot since Korea, too."

Thus far, that was the only glimpse of Rip's past I had. I glanced at the book he'd been reading and saw that it was *The Meditations* of Marcus Aurelia. He followed my glance and explained, "Picked it up in a dump. Good reading."

I told him that for old times sake I was thinking of catching a freight west for a day or so. That was enough to turn Rip into a talking time table of freights heading west. He decided for me that I should take Train No. 222 which was scheduled to leave at 9:13 in the morning. He explained that it was a slow freight, with several half-hour stops, and would probably lay up in Livingston, Montana, several hours in the night. On the positive side, the train had a good natured crew and there were likely to be a number of "broken boxes," his term for partially-loaded, clean, and unsealed box cars.

I thanked him for the information and hospitality and was about to return to my austere hostelry when Rip added, "Tell you what. Be downstairs at the Western run, my inn, or at Sonny's about 9:00 and I'll show you around the yards." So, after further thanks, I returned to the town and bedded down.

The next morning, following a breakfast of coffee and toast, I walked about a bit until, from the direction of the jungle, appeared my worthy Rip. After a bit of small talk he said, "I'll check out the yards for you," and strolled into them. I noticed that he was on first-name basis with both the train crews and the yard crew.

After a ten minute stroll through the yard Rip returned to me with more information that I could have gained in a week. "Yup," he said, "Number 222 will be ready to go in about an hour. It's a slow train; it will have three or four half-hour stops today and lay up most of the night in Livingston. After that, an all-day run to Spokane, arriving there about 4:45. If you're in no hurry that's your best bet." He then added, "The number ten car behind the locomotive sounds good," indicating that it was a "breaker". "Besides, Old Ike is the engineer and I told him he might have a rider."

As we had about forty-five minutes to kill before departure I suggested that he be my guest for coffee, so we adjourned to Sonny O'Dea's where coffee is served in the morning. A young fellow was in charge whom Rip called by name. A pleasant welcome was extended.

It was following our cup of coffee together that the real mystery of Rip began to emerge. When I went to pay, Rip said, "No," and pulled out his own billfold instead. I suggested that we match to decide on who would pay. We matched and Rip lost so he paid and it was then I noticed out of the corner of my eye that his partially open wallet was chockfull of a goodly number of bills—Not just Ones either—and a rather thick detachable pocket containing a small sheatf of cards and pictures. I would have given a good deal to examine the wallet but I had already learned from Rip that one would learn from Rip what Rip wanted one to know about him—and that was damned little.

When it was about time to leave, Rip said, "I'll walk down to the yards with you." We reconnoitered our train where Rip pointed out for me car number ten. We encountered a yard crew of four men who were going about their duties and Rip engaged the foreman in conversation. I couldn't hear what they talked about, but as we parted the foreman said, "Hell, no, Rip. I didn't see anybody." This comment only served to heighten the mystery of Rip for me.

Rip pointed out "my" car and was about to explain door etiquette—how to open it discreetly, when to have it closed, and when to have it completely open (thereby converting the

Pullman into an observation car)—when, all of a sudden, he said, "Hell, I might as well go with you. You might need help." He then expertly opened the door a couple of feet, surveyed the contents of the car, and pronounced it suitable. Upon entering, I found that our carriage was more than adequate, half-full with large bales of the type of packing material that one usually finds scattered about after opening Christmas presents.

Just as Rip pronounced it "four stars" we felt the tremor of the power plants—four diesel engines—being revved up. "Until we clear the yards, leave it closed," Rip said as he closed the door. Soon we felt movement and then acceleration. After waiting a few minutes he cracked open the door and peered out. He then opened the door all the way and locked it into position. "It's ours till Livingston!" he announced and so merrily we rolled along, across the high plains and foothills. We stopped three times, I believe, to wait for the more urgent east bound trains to pass. Twice we dismounted, once for beer and once for coffee and sandwiches. Both times, when I went to pay, Rip insisted that we match for it. Both times he lost and paid up. The mystery of my good traveling companion continued to deepen.

Towards evening we sided at Livingston, our last stop of the day. We dismounted and Rip walked up and had a few words with the crew. He returned with two and the information that we could stay until morning. "Let's tour the town," he suggested, "But you'd better take your bag. Some damned yard boss might put a seal on our car."

We went uptown, walked about a bit, and had a modest meal in a modest eatery at a modest price. This time I finally lost the match. As dusk arrived, we returned to our hotel. The car hadn't been locked, so we entered, and arranged our beds of soft, clean bales. Rip then closed the door expertly, jamming the lock with a piece of wood. We talked a bit in the total darkness and then fell into a comfortable sleep.

We were awoken by the slight tremor of our boudoir. Rip's voice came to my ear through the inky miasma: "They're starting to hook up. It will be another fifteen minutes." Shortly thereafter he arose and cracked open the door to full early daylight. He told me that another power unit was being added for the trip through the high mountains. Soon we moved out and Rip opened our sleeper door to reconvert it into a private observation car.

As we progressed to the West through breath-taking scenery and spectacular railroad switch backs, we stopped two or three times at sidings, each time partaking of coffee and a sandwich and beer that we split between us. Each time, at Rip's insistence, we matched for them and he always lost.

Try as I might, I wasn't able to get through Rip's crust but it seems that in his memory there were only two periods of time, "Before Korea" and "After Korea." Beyond that, nothing. He seemed to have an adequate formal education and had read widely if randomly. I also surmised that Rip had some sort of assured but modest income, probably a pension relating to the Korean War. As to the reason for his lifestyle, I could only guess that it had to relate to some traumatic experience suffered during the Korean War or, upon his homecoming, thereafter. At any rate, he seemed to have led this wondering life ever since Korea yet still maintained a wry sense of humor and his self respect, evidence of which was that he was scrupulously neat and clean.

We arrived at Spokane's large freight yard about 4:30 PM. As I intended to resume hitchhiking in the morning, it was time to part company with Rip. I insisted, however, that he be my guest at our last supper. He reluctantly agreed and led the way to a small train-crew eatery across the way.

We sat at a small table and ordered a small meal. While eating I suggested to Rip that inasmuch as I intended to get a room in one of the small cheap hotels hereabout, I would get a double and he could be my guest.

With some hesitation he said, "No. Think I'll take the night flight home," meaning a freight train east.

Earlier in the day, when sort of feeling out my companion, I had asked Rip what the weather around here was like in the winter. It was a sort of a question, but indirect. He returned with an answer that was just as indirect. "Don't really know, but the peppers are really good down along the Rio Grande."

When our second coffee arrived, I finally asked Rip directly, "Why in the name of God, don't you quit this wandering and settle down?" His answer will always be engraved in my memory: "Well, I'll tell you, John, after Korea I just wanted to get away for a while and it sort of grows on you. Now I guess I just want to be where I aint." With that he excused himself to go to the rest room. I watched him go in and come out and then, not unexpectantly for some reason, turn and walk out the back door into the darkness.

Indonesian Holiday

👍

Friday, October 23, 1992

Log book of the good ship, Lollipop, captained by the doughty old sea dog John A. McGlynn, Jr. Hereinafter, the old bugger will appear in the log as "Cap." The crew, enlisted at various water fronts are as follows:

Second Mate	Carp Rockweiler
Chief Cook	Carp Rockweiler
He Who Must Obey	Carp Rockweiler
Crew of the Captain's Gig	Carp Rockweiler
Boson's Mate	Carp Rockweiler
General Gofer	Carp Rockweiler

The crew, in this log, will, henceforth be referred to collectively as "Carp." The company of adventurers who organized this voyage of discovery were incorporated under the name "Annie's Progeny."

Cap's orders (sealed), were to sail in a westerly direction into the great unknown. It seems that the spouses were evenly divided as to whether the world was round or flat. Cap, to tell the truth, is of the opinion that both views are in error. From decades of adventures on the high seas, and possessing a keen and analytical mind, he is convinced that terra firm and terra incognita form a slightly bulging equilateral triangle, with each angle of the said triangle properly dubbed as "the point of no return." Whatever the case may be, this heroic voyage will provide a definitive answer to questions that have bedeviled geographers since the memory of man runneth not to the contrary.

Another reason for this epic is, if possible, to track down said progeny's long-lost brother, John Hubert. Some are of the opinion that he has been devoured, after being properly stewed and spiced, by a jolly crew of cannibals. Others are of the opinion that while stumbling around in the dark, he tripped over a county line and fell off the edge of the flat earth. If such is the case he is probably in orbit, and will be for eternity or maybe longer.

Another and more attractive possibility is that the prodigal has cornered the trade of the Spice Isles and is lolling about in the midst of a vast and lustful harem. At any rate, crusty old Cap will return with answers to all questions. His report will be the truth, the whole truth, and damned little of that.

Naturally, both Cap and all his numerous crew hope that the fate of the missing prodigal is contained in the third option, for the following reasons, that John Hubert will, from the goodness of his heart take in the weary Argonauts, give them a night's lodging, some warm beer, and send them away laden with gifts: namely a shipload of pepper and a dozen or so spares from his harem. But, come to think of it, that is a hell of a lot of pepper.

But enough of these digressions and back to the serious business of Cap reporting to his stockholders.

His crew was shaped up thusly. The boson mate, on Cap's orders, summoned the motley crew to the poop deck where Cap lectured with great severity. In a voice as that from the tomb,

Cap gave his orders of sailing. As each article — There were seventeen of them, each ending with the phrase, "The penalty of any transgression of the Cap's orders shall be death or such other penalty as Cap may direct"— the crew was soon in a state of abject obedience. Seeing this, Cap, severe old sea dog that he is, asked if there were any questions. After a long and pregnant silence, a member of the crew of the captain's gig raised his hand and asked Cap in a thunderous voice, "You damned old fool, just who do you think you are?" Cap, crusty old mariner that he is, stammered a bit and answered in a most authoritative manner, "Damned if I know!"

Shortly after, Cap and crew donned cowboy boots and danced the polka. Thus was iron discipline established. But enough of this. On the morrow, Cap and crew will weigh anchor in the snug harbor of Glynnspring and steer toward the land of the setting sun. Whether they return in triumph, or return at all, only God knows, and I think He's in doubt.

But enough of this prologue. On the flowing tide the travelogue begins, inevitably followed by the epilogue. And so to bed...

Monday, October 26

Weighed anchor at 6:30 A.M. and, with Carp, the crew, at the wheel and Captain on the bridge, headed our good ship on course to Kansas City, Missouri. The journey was uneventful but interesting. Our first difficulty: that fool of a Carp sailed through a speed zone in Fennimore, Wisconsin, the net result of which was that he was relieved of sixty-nine dollars. The Captain gave him a royal tongue lashing and threatened to throw him overboard. Being properly chastised, he proceeded on course, now at a more moderate speed. Nothing of great import occurred from thence to Kansas City. We arrived at the home of Luke, tenth in the line of progeny, just as he returned from work. Gratefully, we found both natives—Luke and his wife, Nicole—to be very friendly and welcoming. We spent a very enjoyable evening talking of forgotten lore, getting on the outside of a sumptuous dinner of Luke's creation, and listening to Carp and Nicole discuss matters artistic. (As this journery begins, I find myself more and more impressed with my crew's native intelligence, his self-obtained knowledge of geography, and his damned unstoppable verbosity.)

After each of us had consumed a couple of bottles of Luke's home-brewed beer, it was time for bed.

Tuesday, October 27

Captain and crew arose at the ungodly hour of 5:30 A.M.—Luke had to be off to work at 6:00—and one and all filled their insatiable bellies with free food, the Captain's thinking being that it would probably be quite some time ere we find another shore populated with such well-supplied and generous savages.

Heading on a course 270 degrees West, we crossed the state of Kansas. Some weary travelers would probably say that the less said of Kansas the better, but there is a certain grandeur to the flat and endless plains.

We stopped at every point of interest, and my crew, being an avid photographer and recording nut—VCR, PDQ, or whatever you might call the fool things—recorded and snapped all said points of interest, which were surprisingly many in number. At the setting of the sun we found ourselves in a little town named Cheyenne Wells, Colorado. We did of necessity rent a room at the best, and only, motel in town and thereafter located the town's only eating place which was, not quite unsurprisingly, very close by. And so we fed and now to bed...

Up bright and early and off to the west. Traveled all day in beautiful mountain country, with Carp again using up huge quantities of film. Crossed the High Rockies at Monarch Pass (elev. 12,000 feet). On descending, through more beautiful country, we developed tire trouble and limped into Montrose, Colorado, where a new tire and windshield wipers were purchased. Located a motel, something to eat, and then to bed.

Left Montrose and, traveling on seldom used roads, drove through some of the most breathtaking scenery that I have ever seen in North America—and I've seen a great deal of it. The road, or roads—mostly the secondary type—led over Red Mountain Pass; through the old mining towns of Ouray, Silverton and Durango; thence to Cortez, Colorado. Carp shot an unbelievable amount of pictures and film which will, undoubtedly, provide a valuable record of our safari, but in my mind, his habit of shooting absolutely everything that moves and doesn't move, is getting to be a bit too much.

We stayed the night in a too expensive motel, but we had no choice for deer and elk hunters had filled the town. After something to eat, some writing, and some telephoning, the day was done, and so to bed.

Left Cortez at about 8:00, again on less-traveled roads, and again spent the day traversing some most awesome scenes of natural wonders. As usual our progress was slowed by Carp's filming and by several side trips to unusual and off-the-beaten-path spots of scenic or historic interest. Toward mid-afternoon the weather suddenly turned ugly, and then, quite rapidly, grew more ugly until when we were at an altitude of 10,000 feet, a snowstorm hit. Fortunately, we were descending the mountain by this time. At about 7,000 feet the snow turned to rain and we groped our way for fifty or sixty miles to a point where our course indicated—indeed demanded—a westerly tack. However, at the intersections of both westward-leading roads, the police had set up roads blocks due to the blizzard conditions. In this 10,000 foot-high mountain pass I suddenly had visions of the Donner Party of infamy and started to size up my crew as to his edibility. But as in all such melodramas the Lone Ranger came galloping to our rescue, this time in the form of a neon sign that spelled out "MOTEL." It turned out to be a wee hostelry with one available room; a small grocery was attached and so, rationed and quartered, we are now ready to weather the storm, till hell freezes over, if necessary. The name of this port in the storm is Mount Carmel Junction. And so to bed...

Throughout the night the harsh elements of snow, sleet, and wind, we later learned, continued their attack, but this did not prevent us from sleeping soundly. Suddenly, however, around sun-up, when we did arise, the storm surrendered to the solar rays, whereupon the most awesome landscape that one could imagine was revealed. The mountain peaks, canyons, and vertical escarpments were all clothed in virgin snow. The bright sunlight made the drive through Zion National Park an experience that I have no doubt is beyond the possibility of description. We then proceeded in a generally westerly direction across that vast but impressive wasteland known as Nevada. All this time my crew was busy taking pictures and shooting film of all points of interest and beauty.

Per plan, at around the time that darkness fell, we arrived at the western portal of Yosemite National Park and, not surprisingly, found the passage was closed by blizzard. By necessity, we stayed the night in the town of Lee Vining. On the morrow we shall thus have to detour around this section of the High Sierras if we are to reach our next safe harbor, the home of Colleen, progeny number eight, by sundown.

Sunday, November 1

At first light, I summoned my crew to the poop deck and dressed them down as is my wont, and, leaving them properly chastised, gave them the orders of the day, which were to proceed on a generally westward course and arrive at Colleen's at about four in the afternoon.

During our rather leisurely procession of this day's journey we, Captain and crew, progressed through some three hundred miles of lovely landscape. My calculations were slightly off, however, and we arrived at Colleen's about 5:28 P.M. where——May the gods be thanked!—we were welcomed not only by Colleen but by Mary, progeny number four, as well.

After a sumptuous meal, cooked and served by a well-known chef, that being Colleen, we lay our powerful frames to rest. Having traveled this day and seen many miles of beauty, from the High Sierras to the lush vineyards of Napa Valley, the Captain will now take his daily ration of rum. And so to bed...

This day scheduled, as the British navy would put it, for rest and refit. And it was! As it was Colleen's day off, she was free to give us a cook's tour of the area. We went and looked over the house she is about to move into, but due to some utility company glitch we were not able to be of much help to her, a fact that brought no great grief to Captain or crew. From thence to a lovely ex-Presbyterian Monkery. It seems the monks had become more adept at debauchery than meditation and so had been turned out to pasture. The place is now a conference center for any group willing to pay the price. A beautiful setting. Thence to the winery of a friend of Colleen's, who is a resident major domo. We were given a tour and more or less had the run of the place but then were forced to critique several of the winery's choice vintages. The chore was long and arduous, it being necessary to get on the outside of several bottles to give an educated critique. We then pronounced them to be of equal excellence or fruitiness, or whatever we experts are supposed to say. Back to Colleen's for a catered gourmet meal which included some more fine vintage. Fearing that the crew would stray from the path of duty, the Captain gave them a severe verbal chastisement and, to keep them in line, forced himself to consume the temptation. A very heavy load it was for the old sea dog to bear, but duty is duty. And so to bed...

Election Day dawned. We repacked our bags and left Colleen's house, thereafter stopping in Healdsburg at Samba Java, Colleen's brainchild of a restaurant, for sustenance. After bidding fond farewell to progeny number eight, we then headed south, driving at a leisurely place towards the next port, the home of Mary and her husband Rick, in Redwood City. We took Old Highway No. 1 along the coast, visited Muir Woods, and arrived at Mary and Rick's at about 2:00 P.M. There, we found them, including their daughter Kate, in good skin and feeding, and were greeted most affectionately. After dining at a local Italian restaurant we returned and watched the election results—a changing of the guard. And then to bed...

Wednesday, November 4

Spent the night at Mary and Rick's and, with them having to go about their daily occupation, my crew and I were left more or less to our own devices until it was time for us to depart for unknown regions to the west. After a breakfast of our own creation we settled down to an hour or two of digesting the pontificating of various windbags, known as political analysts or pundits, on TV. I think that the unemployment rolls will swell appreciably now that the election is over and there's no more use for their so-called "services." We also digested our breakfast. Shortly it was time to depart for the San Francisco airport, and so we did.

At 4:00 P.M. we took off for L.A. After landing in L.A. and going through the usual rigmarole and a wait of two hours, we embarked on a five and a half hour flight to Honolulu. After debarking, getting our baggage, getting a cab—The cabby gave us our first indication of the larceny that seems to lurk in the hearts of such Hawaiian tradesmen—and making our way to the hotel it was 4:30 A.M. San Francisco time. A short night, or a long day... And so to bed...

Thursday, November 5

After a short night's sleep—I can't sleep after the sun comes up—Captain and crew sallied forth to look over the terrain. Had coffee and rolls, then parted, Crew to photograph everything in sight and I to observe the so-called humanity lolling in the sands of Waikiki Beach. The majority of the mammals basking in front of the numerous US$ 250 a day rooms in these warrens of the nouveau riche seemed to be fat and fatuous females with fearsome fannies whose sole object in life seems to be to impress others of that damnable ilk. After viewing this sad scene for some time the Captain did more and more agree with Swift's Gulliver, to wit, "The more I see of people the more I love horses."

Following this we went to Pearl Harbor, mainly to the memorial to the dead entombed in the sunken battleship Arizona. I, on the whole, was disappointed, partly I supposed because I expected too much, and partly because the tide was at flow and thus made it difficult to picture what it was and what it might have been.

On this excursion we used nothing but city buses, which is the way to go in this town. The price is low and the drivers, one and all that we met, are most helpful; the whole metropolitan area can be covered thoroughly and at minimum cost. Upon returning from this safari Captain and crew partook of an oriental meal. Thai, I think. Captain gave the whole crew leave to get a taste of nightlife of this friendly port. Cap, as always, true to duty, went to his cabin and ink-stained wretch that he is, is finishing his daily log. And then to bed...

Friday, November 6

Cap awoke at sunrise and piped his crew on deck. After a light breakfast we, after a half-hour wait, boarded a sightseeing bus, or rather a van, for a projected circumnavigation of the island of Oahu. It turned out to be a delightful trip, the reason for the euphoria of the whole thing was due in part to the scenic and historical grandeur of the island, but just as important was the congeniality and cosmopolitanism of our fellow flatland touristers. The total number was nine, including ourselves. One was from England, two from California, two from Utah, one from Texas, and one from Canada. Our driver, a 100% native Hawaiian, was very articulate and congenial, all in all a very pleasant and educational day.

Returned to our hotel area about 5:00 P.M., showered, listened to the news and weather, then sallied forth to search out an evening meal. The meal we found at a sidewalk thievery called "The Pot Bellied Pig." I then returned to the room and read the paper. My crew (Carp) headed for the beach to film the sunset. Methinks this budding Cecil B. DeMille must have used up several miles of film by now. Oh well, to each his own thing... And so to bed...

Saturday, November 7

On this day Captain and crew arose at a late hour, did our usual ablutions. Had a reasonably good breakfast at a "reasonably" priced thievery up the street. After a severe verbal chastisement, the crew was given shore leave for the day, and one and all took off in all directions at once.

Old Cap, after considerable cogitation, decided to pull a Doctor Jekyll and Mr. Hyde act, the Hyde in this case was to be transferred, in persona, to a reporter for some unnamed mainland periodical. Thusly transformed, pen and notebook in hand, I proceeded down the two or three miles of Waikiki Beach. I found that almost without exception everyone of the basking sharks just loved to be interviewed, thinking that their names will be engraved in the headlines of my slick periodical, which I assured them, would appear in the "Scientific Journal of Mid-America." I found that almost all interviewees were damned near as phony as their interviewer. Upon completion of my duty as a wandering journalist I did retransform myself to Dr. Jekyll and boarded a metropolitan bus for sixty cents without asking its destination. It turned out that said destination was a well-known surfing beach on the north coast of this island. After some twenty minutes of BS-ing with other wandering albatrosses–Or should it be albatri?– boarded another bus for Waikiki. The bus drivers of this island are most friendly and articulate, as are the gendarmes, carabrini, police force, or whatever. After returning to the general area of our hotel, I was at this point apprehended by a jolly minion of the law for jaywalking. Called by Badge Hawaii 50, believe it or not, the connotation being this is the fiftieth state. He more or less said that as he was going off duty and that he had to have some paper work to do. All this violent transgression meant that I initialed a sheet and gave him proof that he was doing his duty.

Inasmuch as he was getting off duty, and the branch police station was just across the street, I invited him to our room for a bit of refreshment (My crew had left a jug of Jim Bean!). He accepted the invite with alacrity and our uniformed minion of the law proved to be a most congenial and interesting fellow. After getting on the outside of a generous quota of bourbon, he left and, after mutual protestations of affection, on his departure he assured me that any transgression other than murder and bank robbery would be seen with a blind eye.

About this time the sun was setting in the west (as usual). My trusty crew returned from wherever, and by mutual agreement we went out for a bite. After returning from the local thievery, watching the evening news, and reading a paper stolen from the lobby, my crew and I prepared for well-deserved repose. On the morrow my crew will, with the Captain's permission, go on an inter-island tour. The ancient mariner who pens this log will go to mass. There is a church but two or three blocks from here. Without doubt the priest will wear a hula skirt and the altar boys will be shilling for tour companies. The human race, I fear, is going to hell in a hand basket. The gloomy dean, I fear, had the right attitude: The more I see of people the more I love horses. But again, judge not lest ye also be judged. But 'tis the last day on these scenic isles. And so to bed...

Sunday, November 8

Awoke as late as possible this morning anticipating a long day, as were scheduled to fly out at midnight and will be approximately eighteen hours en route, so there will be very little rest. On looking around I found that my whole damned crew had jumped ship. I was furious until I remembered that I had given Carp permission to visit some other islands to view active volcanoes and some ancient native shrines. I do swear that man has an insatiable curiosity about things geographical and cultural, which is a good and healthy thing, but it does make it difficult to keep track of him. As for myself, I watched a little football — In Hawaii, Sunday football is at 7:00 A.M. — then took a self-guided city bus tour of the city and its environs, stopping at the state capital which I found rather interesting.

Carp eventually returned from his day of volcanism. A bit late, but we still had ample time to get to the airport, fill out some forms for international flight, and board our plane which for some reason took off an hour late. We have no expectation of bed this night and little of sleep. And so ends the day.

Monday, or Tuesday, depending on the international date line, we took off from Honolulu at about 2:00 A.M. on a clear moonlit night. After reaching altitude, we could see below us areas of moonlit floating clouds but mostly vast reaches of black Pacific. After an hour of staring out the window at this scene I was reminded of Ben Franklin's statement that in the dark all black cats look alike. So, after checking the behavior of my crew, I settled down to do some writing, bringing this log up to date and starting to write a letter to my lawfully wedded spouse and to each of her numerous offspring—more time at putting pen to paper in one session than this doughty old mariner has ever done before, methinks. This occupation was interrupted every so often—it seemed more often than so—by refreshments or a full meal. Apparently, Garuda Indonesian Airways has a worldwide reputation for fighting hunger.

Inasmuch as we were chasing the setting moon and fleeing the rising sun, the night was inordinately long. We crossed four or five time zones. By the time dawn had caught us we were approaching our first stop—Biak, in extreme eastern Indonesia.

The stop was for fuel but one or two passengers did debark and one or two boarded. Biak is a leftover outpost of World War II and appears to have has changed but little since that time. Our next stop was Bali, which was apparently the primary destination of this intercontinental flight, as 90% of the passengers did there debark, most of them on their first trip out of the United States. They envisioned a Pacific paradise but really landed in a neon-lit tourist trap. From thence to Jakarta, some one and a half hours.

We had expected that John would be there to meet us, but no John. Finally, after sometime I managed to get him on the phone. I was helped in this endeavor by several locals—a couple of girls at an information desk, neither of whom could speak much English. At any rate we did finally manage to get John on the phone. To his total surprise we had arrived a day ahead of his understanding of our plans and ETA the reason being the difference of dates at that time of day.

At any rate we took a cab, or a wild man, to John's ménage and to our surprise arrived in one piece (each) at John's place and were welcomed warmly.

My first impression of Indonesian people is of their extreme politeness and genuine friendliness, except for cab drivers, who from Timbuktu to Timor, are a bunch of thieves. At any rate after a most tasty dinner, served by John's several very polite cooks and house servants, we did partake of several very potable after-dinner drinks. We retired after some thirty hours with little or no sleep. Repose was welcome. And so to bed...

Wednesday, November 11

After sleeping the sleep of the just for some fourteen or fifteen hours I did awake fully refreshed, and found my foolish crew missing. The whole damned bunch had long since gone forth, taking pictures. He reminds me of Christ in the temple. After his return we were served an excellent breakfast, again by the aforementioned servants. Such service is nice, but somehow the obsequiousness of my fellow man makes me a bit sad. We, with John's driver and car, then safaried to the high points of interest in Jakarta, a city larger than New York. Due to a lack of communication—our driver spoke no English and we spoke no Indonesian—some of the high points were missed, but on the whole a most instructive day. Back to our base of operations for another excellent meal and a fortunate meeting with Pramoedya Ananta Toer, one of Indonesia's most famed authors who had served much time in prison We—Carp, John and myself—planned an itinerary for tomorrow's adventures and then to bed...

We, or at least I, did spend the night sleeping the sleep of the just, as if cradled in the arms of the gods. This was probably due to lingering effects of jet lag. At any rate, shortly after sunup there was a discreet knock on the door and an almost invisible servant guided in with coffee and a plate filled with some tropical fruit unknown to me, but tasty and refreshing. After showering and shaving there was another quiet knock and in glided a breakfast of boiled eggs and more tropical fruit, this time transported by John's chief cook and maid, a Javanese lady of indeterminable years, probably well past the half century mark. I'm getting to like this sort of service—I fear too much—for there's a good chance that I will be constrained to fire Mother if she is too noisy or not sufficiently respectful when she serves her lord and master breakfast in bed.

Our car and driver soon arrived and we embarked on a pre-planned tour of things educational and historical, of which this city provides a plethora. The main focus of the day were two:

Number 1 was a tour of the buildings and artifacts of the Dutch East India Company, built largely between 1635 and 1700—these, in the most part, perfectly preserved in the original—which gave one to ponder on man's inhumanity to man. Very impressive and sobering. Number 2, the waterfront with its vast open air market. Foul smelling, filthy, but fascinating. The fish market was all of the above and doubled. Surrounding and surrounded by countless numbers of miserable hovels of people who lived and worked there. In spite of these depressing surroundings, the inhabitants were, without fail, polite and friendly, and the children—of which there seemed to be an endless supply—were, I believe, the happiest group of waifs I have ever seen, a damned sight more so than the dour, spoiled, little brutes that one would see at Disneyland.

The highlight of the day was a two-hour tour of Sunda Kelapa Harbor, wending our way by small boat in and out among the countless inter-island cargo ships, mostly hauling lumber from Borneo (Kalimantan) and God knows what back. Our gondolier, being a friend of one of the ships' captains, obtained permission to board her and gave us the run of the ship. Very instructive and gratifying. Thence back by water to and through the odiferous market and by car home. After a very large and mysterious meal of Javanese cookery, back to the sleeping quarters. After a bit of time to digest the day's adventures, the day ended. And so to bed...

Thursday, November 12

A rather brief entry in this day's log, I hope. After a good night's sleep we arose and after the usual morning ablutions, were again besieged by the near-invisible servants bearing vast quantities of excellent coffee, fruit juices and various other viands. In Carp's case there was a three-course breakfast of eggs, bacon, tofu or whatever. (He claims that this tropical climate makes him gain weight!)

We then embarked on a pre-planned tour of more sights and places of historical and cultural interest. I won't bore you with a rundown of the tour as "everybody" has been to Indonesia. Upon returning to John's we found that he had plans for the morrow—and what plans they were! We are to leave here at the ungodly hour of 1:30 A.M. and are to spend the weekend on an island in the Java Sea owned by friends of John's. Whether I am to be admiral of the fleet or cabin boy I know not. At any rate, Carp and John have sallied forth to lay in supplies for the voyage, and I to an abbreviated repose. And so to bed...

Friday, November 13

Did this night arise at the ungodly hour of 1:30 A.M. and by taxi proceeded to the vast Jakarta waterfront. Somehow found and boarded what was to me at least a palatial yacht, and weighed anchor at about 2:30 A.M. A word about our overgrown row boat: It was seventy feet long and had comfortable cabins for each of the four guests plus an extra large one for the host, together with a complete galley.

It being a beautiful moonlit night, stayed the whole night on deck. The moonlight was brilliant so the horizon and other boats could be seen in bold relief. The sound of very light waves slapping the sides of our noble ark made Cap doze from time to time but Cap was mostly awake, taking in the sights and sounds, an experience not likely to be repeated soon. Shortly after dawn many small islands began to appear, some inhabited and some not. Our host then summoned us to an elaborate breakfast served by a most efficient waiter, dressed for the part.

By this time we were anchored some one quarter mile off our island. There is a reef around the island that makes it necessary to land via a motor-driven dinghy.

We were then introduced to our quarters. Carp and I shared a lovely little bungalow with open sides projecting out over the clear blue sea. We each then, more or less, went our several ways: John and our host out to snorkel on the reef, Carp to sleep, and another guest named Kustomo settled down to some serious drinking. I sallied off to explore this small and primitive island. The total size is not, I think, above forty acres.

After lunch I went swimming in the beautiful coral reef. All went well until I made the mistake of walking into a bed of sea urchins, spiny little devils with numerous and poisonous spikes. The pain was immediate and intense. By the time I reached shore my trusty old feet had swollen to the proportion of pin cushions. On the advice of a native crew member, I sat with feet and legs dangling in the light surf, all the while sipping some excellent brandy. Within an hour or so both the swelling and the pain had pretty much abated.

Toward evening John, Carp and I took the motor dinghy, with a native crewman at the helm, to a fishing village on an island about a mile away. It proved to be most interesting, a place of grinding poverty—beastly crowded, especially with kids, goats, and scrawny chickens—yet the adults were extremely polite and the children happy. It gives one to think....

Back to our island and an excellent dinner, and having had very little sleep for forty eight hours did draw the mosquito netting. And so to bed....

After about twelve hours of deep and peaceful sleep, as if rocked in the cradle of the gods, did awaken, breakfasted and did a little writing, a little reading, and a little lolling about. About noontime we did embark by dinghy to our mother ship, shortly casting off for the return trip to Jakarta. An excellent lunch was served. The return trip was uneventful but interesting. The weather, perfect. Docked at the Ancol marina in Jakarta at dusk. John's car and driver awaited there. Thence home and after planning for the morrow did retire. And so to bed...

Monday, November 16

Did awaken and after breakfasting did try to call Mother, as her birthday was yesterday. I failed to mention that we tried to call her yesterday, but no answer. The same this morning. She must be gone. Carp needed a haircut so John took us to Laris Love, an immense emporium—part barbershop and part barber college.

Inasmuch as John had noticed that my toenails looked like cloven hoofs, he talked me into having a manicure and pedicure. Imagine that! I must admit it was a new and rather pleasant experience. One charming, dusky young lady took charge of my hands, and another my feet. They clipped, filed, dug and massaged the extremities for about an hour. Must admit that both the attention and the results were pleasant. Back to John's and per plan, after lunch we went to Gambir railroad station to board a train to the city of Bandung where we met a man who is supposed to guide us on a tour of the out of the way and primitive parts of Java. To a hotel we went, and soon to bed.

Arose and after usual toilet had an unusual, and expensive, breakfast. The expensive part was largely due to Carp's delusion that he could read a menu in the local lingua. He can't!

Our guide, with car and driver, soon appeared and we set forth on a voyage of discovery, specifically designed by myself, to see the real rural life in this part of Java. It turned out to be most instructive and educational. The countryside surrounding this city consists of mountainous areas of the most intensive agriculture in the world. Rice, rice, and more rice with every little corner that is impractical for rice planted with bananas, cassava, beans, or a row of sweet corn on the narrow dikes between the terraces surrounding the flooded rice paddies—some of them encompassing no more than one tenth of an acre. Here and there are "villages" of probably 100,000 people but ones that take up very little space. All but the main streets are from three to five feet wide, and an unbelievable number of home industries are found there: bakeries, metal workers, haberdashers, etc., each operated by a least three generations, including in-laws and children. Our guide, who was raised in this area, knows exactly how to approach these people. Without exception they welcomed us as they would a long lost loved one. They also loved to have their pictures taken, and in this were accommodated by my crew. As we climbed higher, the main crop turned from rice and vegetables to very small "dairies", then to bamboo, potatoes, tea, tea, and more tea—countless thousands of acres of tea. The vast tea plantations are, it seems, still controlled by the same colonialists that developed them. These same people also seem to control the credit and the agriculture of the area, undoubtedly by way of huge bribes made to the various levels of bureaucrats in this most corrupt of governments.

Egad! Methinks this journal runs on too long, but being commissioned by my company of adventurer's I was given order to submit a full report, and so I shall.

After a full day of such as mentioned above we stopped at a dairy cooperative, again under the control of the colonial tea plantations. A very primitive sort of operation, milking twenty cows. We had to walk one quarter of a mile across an abandoned railroad trestle to get there. All milk has to be carried out the same way. This "dairy", a modern one, is the source of support for an extended family of nine adults, eleven children and six "old ones," people too old to work and unable to die. Here they venerate the old—a very admirable trait, I think.

At the time we were watching the milking operation, the heavens opened and the rains came, and came, and came–probably five inches in an hour or so. One way or another, we survived and the day being nearly done, we returned to the city and our hotel with agreement to leave at some ungodly hour in the morning for further adventures to the east. And so to bed....

Wednesday, November 18

We did this day depart our hotel at the ungodly hour of 5 A.M., the reason for this was that it had been arranged for us to take the first leg of the day's journey on a train through what turned out to be unbelievably awe inspiring mountainous country. The train was so crowded that it would have been impossible to crowd on another person or chicken—yes, there were some of them aboard—but no concern to us, for our trusty guide had arranged for us to ride in the locomotive, presenting us with an unparalleled view and a perfect place for Carp to do his usual photography.

After about a two and a half hour ride through spectacular rice paddies and mountains we detrained at some unnamed town where our driver was supposed to meet us. He was an hour late, but no bother. It was a most primitive and interesting place and we found some passable coffee, thence by back roads in a leisurely manner through the Sundanese region of West Java. This is supposed to be the most unchanged from pre-colonial times, except for the motor vehicle and an exploding population. One village was of particular interest. One had to walk perhaps one quarter mile down a slippery path and stone steps to get there, as did the natives to get in or out. The people still practiced an animistic religion, and probably hadn't seen over a handful of Caucasians in their life; it was a most unusual experience. From there we journeyed hence to find a small and cheap hotel, the only one in town. Am going to try to call John. And so to bed...

Thursday, November 19

Arose after a good night's sleep and after a very good but inexpensive breakfast did depart this city of Tasikmalaya for another tour of back roads and villages in this part of the country. More primitive places and then a most educational tour of one of the biggest rubber and cocoa plantations in the world. We had the run of the place, with a guide whom, I think, was in the employ of the government. In spite of their "official" capacity they expect a tip or, as they say, a slight token of retribution or tip—just another form of corruption rampant in these isles. But Rp. 5,000 is only about US$ 2.50 and was well worth it. We saw the whole shebang: planting, harvesting and processing. From thence to a fantastic four-hour ride on a local ferry boat. The thing was, I suspect, left over from the Russo-Japanese war! It was packed tighter than any sardine can with humanity, along with live chickens, bananas, coconuts, and us. This sea-going coffin stopped at about a dozen fishing villages. At each stop we added and subtracted more humanity, chickens, bananas, dried fish, and you-name-it. Reached the town of Cilacap around dusk where we found lodgings, then bathed and shaved (in cold water) and are about to go find something to eat. And then to bed...

Friday, November 20

Arose this morning to the sound of thunderous rain on the rooftop. It seems this had been going on all night but I, being in the arms of Morpheus, was not aware. After rising and having a light breakfast, the rain stopped abruptly and we departed on our journey of the day. Were diverted and detoured a dozen times by washed-out bridges and flooded highways. It seems that this was a most spectacular rainfall, even by Indonesian standards. A most interesting trip. It showed how well these natives face nature in the raw. They were all out surveying their dangerously flooded rice and vegetable fields along the half-flooded roads, trying to net tiny fish, eels and frogs, which, as I understand, they would add to the rice and call it a delicacy.

The proposed destination was the Buddhist temple and shrine, Borobudur, the largest and, they say holiest, as well as most perfectly preserved shrine in all of Southeast Asia. Surrounded by an impeccably maintained compound, all surrounded by a wall, it is to the Buddhists of this part of the world the same as is Mecca to the world of Islam.

We were fortunate to arrive about 4 P.M. (the grounds are

closed at 5:00 P.M.) and found lodgings inside the compound, a really delightful room surrounded by subservient servants. Inasmuch as we were within the compound, we had the run of the place as long as we wished. Oddly enough, our "guest house," all beautifully appointed, has sixteen units and only three seem to be occupied (by us, our guide, and a dour old Dutchman). Yet each day there are several thousand pilgrims a day who arrive by bus, "do" the place, and depart before darkness falls on the great shrine. I feel that a week would be insufficient to absorb even a small part of the grandeur, history, and beauty of this place. But more of that on the morrow. One more note of incongruity in this incongruous land is that at this moment some Islamic mullah or whatever you call them, is howling up a storm about the greatness of Allah from the minaret of a mosque just across the way. But now the wails of the muezzin die away and the sleep of the just is due. So to bed...

Saturday, November 21

Arose at about 7:00 to the sound of the usual morning downpour. Tried to call John—he usually works in his office one or two hours before breakfast—but the phone system here is a mystery, even to the operators. As usual a "light" was served in our room. This seems to be part of the price of lodging in these isles, no matter what class of hostelry one might find oneself. By the time we had consumed our cold boiled duck egg, a large plate of various fruit, a slice of tapioca bread, and a cup of sickening sweet coffee, the rain had stopped and the sun was breaking through the clouds. Thanks be to Allah!

We then sallied forth to view and study one of the most mysterious, mystifying and awe-inspiring works of man on this old planet. No matter how facile one's pen, or how expert one's photography, it would be an insult to the living Buddha to think you could transport the essence of this place beyond its walls. Briefly, however, the main shrine is a great stepped pyramid consisting of seven tiers. The walls between the tiers are completely covered by intricate bas relief figures that number in the hundreds of thousands, maybe more. Each and every one of them having meaning to a student of the religion. The broad horizontal areas are covered with statues of Buddha in various sizes as well as statues of various symbolic animals. According to the belief of the Buddhists—reincarnation—all of us animals are equal and might come back in the next life in any form. To wit, do not swat a fly for it might be your grandmother.

The upper two horizontal plazas are dominated by seventy-one monstrous stupa, resembling stone bells, or facsimiles thereof, each having numerous diamond-shaped openings, inside of which is a statue of the Buddha. The belief is that if one is able to reach in and touch one of the old bugger's toes, you will be doubly blessed. I hit on two of the seven tries, better odds than a slot machine.

I was fortunate to lose track of Carp and our trusty guide Felix, because I happened upon an aged monkish person who spoke English fluently. (He hailed from India but had been educated at Oxford, England.) He explained to me the obscure meanings of all the multitudinous bas relief figures, as far as my small mind could absorb. Upon being asked when he would complete his studies he answered in a most sincere manner: "Impossible in one life, but maybe in some future reincarnation." Must say that this is all beyond my "practical" mind and that the whole experience left me at once mystified and fulfilled yet somehow diminished.

Upon leaving this wonderland we proceeded to Yogyakarta, a "town" of two million where we found lodgings. Our guide is an absolute genius at bargaining and well worth his modest remuneration just for that. After a dinner of stringy water buffalo steak and a couple of beers with a most convivial Dutch couple, we returned to our modest but clean and comfortable rooms. Finished this entry in this journal for the day. And soon to bed...

Sunday, November 22

Was awakened by a very discreet knock on the door and an almost invisible houseboy glided in with the usual "light" breakfast: tapioca bread, toast, cold boiled duck egg, coconut butter jam, and hot tea in a glass—not my choice, but when in Rome one does as the Romans do. About this time our guide Felix called and announced that he, car, and driver would arrive in five minutes. About forty-five minutes later they did arrive. This is what is called "rubber time." No explanation was given and none expected. Forsooth, I think this is a better way.

Our day's venture had been planned last night. It included the city market, a vast and crowded area filled with stalls selling everything imaginable: live chickens, anemic ducks, dead chickens with feathers still attached, dressed chickens not yet starting to rot, and so on. Thousands and more of these stalls with ten times that many people flowing through the area. The "streets" through the market were about four feet wide and one felt that you went with the flow of a slow but irresistible flood.

After escaping this unbelievable mess we proceeded to tour the partially decayed palace of Sultans Nos. I, II, and III, probably encompassing 160 acres. The harem alone had 530 rooms for his 530 "wives." Yesterday I thought of being reincarnated as a polar bear but am, of the moment, leaning towards taking over a sultanate. But ye gods, 530 wives would, at my age, be at least several too many.

After several more stops, all of historical and cultural interest, we did return to our hostelry and found, thanks be to Allah, that I had some clean laundry (It is done here for less than the cost of the electricity at home!). Will now sally forth with crew and guide to dine, probably over ripe duck eggs, rice and snails, well done, but I find this damned pen now in hand does carry one on too long, I shall cast it aside and find one with less verbosity. And so to bed...

Monday, November 23

Did this day awake to the sound of the usual morning downpour, but as usual within the hour it was over and the sun was shining. Thanks be to Allah! We had tentatively scheduled stops at several points of interest, starting with Imogiri, the tomb of a whole passel of sultans. The place was ten times bigger than we expected, starting with a stairway consisting of some 400—probably one quarter mile in length—all of one half that vertically. After negotiating this, one comes to the mausoleum area, an immense thing and holy as blazes to us followers of the Prophet. It consists of three levels. The first and second are the resting place of Sultans II to X and the top reserved for Sultan II who, in these parts is called "The Great", but more of him later.

Before entering the great gate one has to remove all clothing but shorts and rent a sarong for a pittance. This garment is then attached around the waist by an aged attendant. Then, after a ritual bath—hands, feet, and shoulders—barefooted and bare from the waist up (or, in the case of women, from breast up) we pass through the great gate. At any rate no women are ever allowed to the topmost level. Escorted by a fierce-looking fellow with a wicked-looking dagger in his belt. Our guide Felix was allowed to accompany us and interpret.

Each of the sultans has a large and imposing sarcophagus, sometimes with his number one wife or queen beside him, sometimes not. Some distance away are the resting places of his numerous secondary wives and innumerable children.

The eldest son of the primary wife supposedly succeeded as sultan, but in actuality his chances were not good. It seems that from day one the numerous secondary wives or more numerous concubines of the harem schemed to jockey their sons into position to at least make a run for the sultanate. Needless to say, this put the rightful heir in a precarious position and most of them seemed to die a natural death by poison, strangulation, or an accidental fall from the battlements, or a well-placed dagger. Such little domestic squabbles served two purposes: it left room for promotion, and disgraced number-one wife, as she had failed to protect the true heir. Not a large and happy family. It probably made it beastly hard to get life insurance on the male children of wife number-one.

But enough of this: we now approached the holiest of holies. Now another word about Felix: although a putative Christian (Catholic, that is), he is steeped in all of the religions of this vast region, so although the topmost level is barred to all but true believers he, a natural born actor, convinced the guard and muezzin that he was a true believer and was accompanied by two converts from a far land to commune with the spirit of the Great One. At any rate, we were admitted. (In all probability, Felix slipped a bribe to the captain of the guard.) The entrance to this inner sanctum consists of three very low gates, each guarded by a couple of fierce-looking buggers armed with vicious-looking scimitars.

One has to almost crawl on hands and knees. This rigmarole is symbolic: the Great Sultan in life was approached in this manner and so in death his spirit must be approached in the same manner. On entering the true inner sanctum there is a very small door, almost a tunnel. At the entrance, we true believers kneel with palms together and knock our heads on the sill, muttering some words in Arabic, and crawl into the holiest of holies, second only to Mecca.

Inside, lighted only by two small incense pots, are two holy men. A pilgrim takes the hand of one and prays some unintelligible phrases, then deposits a small offering (i.e. bribe) in a brass pot. (Felix had instructed us to secret a few small bills in our sarongs.) For that offering, the pilgrim is given a small bunch of flower petals which are gently pressed into his hand. These are to be placed on the sarcophagus of the Great One. The pilgrim then backs out of this shrine The reason that he goes out backwards is that it is forbidden—in life or death—to show the Great One ones backside. Then out to the blessed sunlight... Let Allah be praised! My poor crew, Carp, due to his pot belly, had a bit of difficulty, but finally, like the cork from a child's play gun, popped out. Then in a straight line back to the great portal and my blessed shoes—May Allah be praised!—the rest of our clothes, and Carp's cameras.

I failed to mention that no cameras, writing or sketching materials are allowed beyond the great portal.

At any rate down we descended those several hundred steps and another half mile of precipitous paved pathway to the car. The hour was growing late and the evening downpour threatened, so we decided to forgo any further adventures and return to our hotel. (The hotel itself is worth a page in this journal, but I shall desist.)

But, one more paragraph, if your patience permits, about our great sultan. He is revered for several reasons: First, he more or less fought a successful war against the Dutch colonialists for some thirty years and, in the process, did catch and make mincemeat out of couple governors general, several major generals, and a bevy of lesser dignitaries, for which he deserves the praise of Allah. This was between 1630 and 1660 A.D.

To keep his troops and followers happy in the off season, he would lead them out to "convert" the local and peaceful Buddhists and Hindus to the true faith, i.e., Islam. His method was simple and effective—round up a few thousand of them at a time and give them a choice: either accept the Koran or within five minutes be sliced up and used to fertilize the rice fields. Due to their sincere belief in reincarnation, probably 50% took the latter course, and were dispatched to a life, better or worse. Maybe come back as a lesser Buddha, maybe a water buffalo, maybe a snail. The other 50% became followers of the Prophet, for which Allah be praised.

Another of his accomplishments was to acquire a harem of 164 wives and concubines and father about 180 children, a sign of the true greatness—for which Allah be praised. But enough of the Great One.

My guide and crew (Carp) have gone out pub crawling and I, alone and unwanted, shall partake of a light dinner of snail and coconut soup, try to call John, and then wrap myself in the arms of Allah for the night.

105

Awoke, as usual, to the sound of the rain, but, as usual, by the time the breakfast was done, the rain stopped and we were off to our day's adventures. The first was, I fear, a misadventure. Having some time last night, being the fine fellow I am, I wrote thirteen postcards—Imagine the labor!—and having stamps in hand did inquire at the desk as to the correct postage. I was assured it was eight hundred rupiah. Such was duly attached and cards posted. Later in the day on stopping at a post office I saw it posted "Postal cards overseas, Rp. 1,000," so if these cards are in the hands of the prophet, thanks be to Allah.

We made several stops at minor attractions. One was a batik manufacturing emporium—a very extended family enterprise with probably one hundred workers, each having one particular specialized role, and each an artist in his or her own right. (True batik is produced in only four or five places, each by such an extended family and the secrets of their art passed on from generation to generation.) Another was the workplace of a manufacturer of shadow puppets, known as *wayang kulit*. (John, in a former incarnation was deeply interested in this art form.) From thence to another stupendous and stupefying complex of temples known as Prambanan, part Hindu and part Buddhist. It is absolutely unbelievable in size and two-thirds in ruins, which in some ways makes it even more impressive.

The people of this area are an odd mixture: eighty percent call themselves followers of Islam, but retain many of the beliefs and rituals of the Hindus and Buddhists. They were converts of the swords of the great sultan. Until the end of Dutch colonialism the Hindu caste system was still in effect. It made it easier for the Dutch to rule and plunder. The caste system, although out-lawed for the past forty-five years, still lingers. It makes one a little sad to see decrepit old men or women step off the path and bow as one passes, but our guide, Felix, assured us that this is passing away. I certainly hope so, for it seems to me to be one of the most hellish hypocrisies that any so-called religion foisted on thine fellow man. I guess I'm too democratic.

After leaving the great temple, we went to tea at, of all places, a Burger King located just outside the grounds. Truly a land of contrasts. After leaving the temple area fully con-fused as to the religions of this confusing area, we did, after numerous stops for my crew to photograph water buffalos at work and workers in the numerous small tobacco fields here-about, we spent some time at a most immense and old-fash-ioned sugar refinery. The machinery was huge: old steam en-gines built in Holland and Germany before 1885 were still functioning perfectly. The inefficiency of the place was obvi-ous, but labor is so cheap here that it would fly in the face of economics to be efficient. This plant claims to turn out four thousand 200-pound bags of sugar per day. This is but one of many such refineries in this area, and yet Indonesia still has to import sugar. The reason for this, I think, is that if you don't stop a waiter he will spoil a perfectly good cup of coffee with at least a shovelful of sugar.

We then proceeded to the ancient city of Surakarta, known also as Solo, and found the lodgings where I am now ensconced. The day is about to draw to a close and this log may have no further entry. But as we are about to sally forth with our trusty Felix to sup in an oriental manner, the closure shall be withheld.

Having supped and, with nothing of great note having

transpired, other than running into a couple of rather unsavory American tourists, the type that always put their worst foot forward, I will bid good night...

Wednesday, November 25

Awoke, did our usual ablutions and had the usual hotel breakfast—coffee or tea, two slices of toast with great gobs of jam, and either juice or a great plate of tropical fruit. The well-planned day's activities started out well but ended a fiasco. It seems that the unexpected is to be expected in these remote isles. First was a trip to the site of Java Man, whom one school of anthropologists are sure is the source of all wisdom on the evolution of Homo Erectus. Another school swears by African sources, and still another by Peking Man. Only Allah knows and He ain't telling. At any rate we went there expecting to find easy access, but no. There is a rather interesting government-built museum at the entrance to the area, but the actual area of discovery and dig site entails a walk of two or three miles through steamy jungle and on precarious paths atop the terraces between rice paddies. As long as we had gone that far we went the whole distance, but the site itself was rather a disappointment. But then neither of us is a gung-ho anthropologist. It was surprising, though, the number of bone fragments and teeth of our ancestors there were scattered about the rice and peanut fields. We returned to the city of Solo from whence we came, checked out of the hotel. Had lunch and then called on a money changer.

We then went to a most remote and mystifying and monumental shrine, temple, or whatever in this land of anomalies. The temple, Candi Sukuh, which was built in the fifteenth century, is partly Hindu, partly Buddhist and partly the ancient animistic beliefs of the original Javanese. How in the name of Allah they created these structures: immense stones, great ribbons of bas relief, is beyond me. Only Allah knows and He's in doubt.

Then began the fiasco: Our trusty guide Felix took a precipitous road, supposedly through an area of active volcanoes and unbelievable scenery. After some hours of ascending, this four-wheel drive goat that Felix was driving drove past a rather obscure sign saying "Road Probably Closed." It was. It seems that the government had decided it would be wise to blast a new path for lava threatening the part of the "highway." As a result of this they managed to blow some several thousand boulders as large as a piano onto the roadway. It was definitely closed. After some minutes of maneuvering we got turned around and started to retrace our way... But, lo and behold, a recent landslide blocked our way. So there we were. Fortunately, there appeared as if from nowhere a veritable horde of natives armed with rice hoes and other primitive tools. In no time at all they had the roadway sufficiently open for us to make our escape. But then, to add to our tribulations, our trusty Felix got hopelessly lost on minor mountain roads, as night and rain did fall. This state of affairs called for drastic action. So your crusty old Cap did chastise Felix, telling him "By the beard of the Prophet if you do not set a true course for safe harbor, I shall have your ears cut off, your tongue slit, and the hairs of your beard plucked out, one at a time, all to the greater honor of Allah. Furthermore," I said, "may the Dutch return and reenslave your children! Thus chastised, did Felix find his way out of the labyrinth to a fair-sized city where we are now ensconced in a rather too expensive hotel, but the only one in town. And so ends a rather frustrating day...

After a short night's sleep, due to our late arrival, after traveling mountain-goat trails in the dark and rain last night, so spent the bulk of the day in actual travel, trying to catch up. Nonetheless managed to do several things of interest, in addition to viewing beautiful scenery. One point, to me at any rate, was a large cattle market in the foothills where cattle are more common and a family's wealth may be measured in the number of head of Brahman cattle or buffalos one might own. Over two head and you're a climbing capitalist. I forgot to mention that goats and sheep are of some, but lesser, value on the economic ladder. This is not a cattle sale as we know it, but more or less of a bazaar where individuals dicker with others as to price and weight. Some are trades between owners with differing needs, and it seems many of the owners lead, or more likely, drive the beasts to market just to socialize and to get a free appraisal of their wealth by the bids they receive. They then hitch them to their carts and drive them home. The whole of the sales ground is surrounded by and split with innumerable hawker stands, selling everything from fried chicken entrails to bull whips: a most interesting view of a different culture.

Upon arriving at this town of Malang, we found a vacation home, presently unoccupied, belonging to a sister of our trusty (?) guide Felix. Soon after checking out the place and leaving our bags, we went to a shrine for Hindu, Buddhist, and Chinese-ancestor-worship rituals, but mostly the latter, or so it seems. Their main rituals are performed at night every thirty-fifth day. The main ritual consists of an ancient Chinese man sacrificing a young goat by cutting his throat in a most savage manner. At this time all the assembled Chinese and many of other faiths (including yours truly) light candles, sticks of incense, and mutter some unintelligible lingo to the spirits: Chinese, Hindu, Buddhist, and one Irishman. Somebody's late grandmother must have been really ticked off that night, for at that moment the heavens opened and the damnedest downpour you ever did see came down. We had to walk down a half-mile ramp and set of steps to our car. It was raining so hard we could almost swim. After wringing ourselves out we drove some forty kilometers back to our digs where we found the lights to be out. Not uncommon in these parts. If I learned anything from this ritual it is, don't even think about your ancestors. And so groped my way to bed...

Friday, November 28

Did sleep late this A.M., partly from need of sleep and partly because Felix had sent our soaked clothes off with some semivisible servant to be dried. His drier was a new family invention call the clothesline. Fortunately the machine worked and by about 9:30 we were back in presentable condition. We then left our free lodgings and returned to the city of Malang for a late breakfast and to have a look at IKIP-Malang, the teachers' college where John once studied. Very nice.

Felix took me to a telephone office to try to call John but it seems the inter-city telephone service is no more effective than ancestor worship. It took seven or eight operators about one half hour to tell me that the connection to Jakarta was "not well. So very very sorry." At least they were polite.

An hour or so late by this time, we started out to what is supposed to be one of the highlights of this trip, a visit to the vast area of active volcanoes—which are very active right now—around Mount Bromo.

The jojourn started out nicely, that is until Felix decided the car needed servicing and pulled into a little garage.... Am now sitting on some friendly Indonesian's porch while across the street are six or eight mechanics trying to decide whether to jack up the hind wheel or to open the hood. God only knows what they'll do after they have voted on this. I think I'll go over to see if they need help breaking a tie vote.

At last a consensus is reached: they do both, the net result being that Carp solved the whole thing by pointing out that the front suspension was out of alignment. A few simple turns of a couple of nuts and all was well. It proves there's still something to be said for American know-how. Then off to the mountain...

The route was one of the most spectacular drives imaginable; it dwarfed anything that the Rocky Mountains have to offer. The last four miles had to be made by four-wheel drive jeep, and that was rather hairy.

We are now ensconced in Bromo Indah Permai, a very comfortable government-run hostel on the very lip of a most tremendous prehistoric crater, an almost vertical drop of about one quarter mile from our door. The floor and walls of this vast arena are spotted with dozens of small and very active craters. Each of them have steam gushing from them and now and then will toss up a curtain of red hot rocks.

It was dusk when we arrived and darkness has now fallen. The whole scene is simply beyond description, but I'm sure Dante must have seen it before he wrote his epic.

The tentative plan is to arise at 3:30 A.M. and walk about four miles in the dark across the mother crater to the largest of the new and active ones. The idea of this whole thing is, it seems to be, to see and film the sunrise. It seems to be a bunch of tomfoolery to me and I shall not be party to it. My experience has always been that mountain sunrises are most spectacular with the sun at ones back, which it will be from this place. What Carp's course will be I know not. At any rate, if the weather permits, mine old eyes will see a sight reserved for very few. If it is clear tonight the moonlight might make it well worth missing some sleep. I will now go to a little food stand near here, and then either to moonlight or to bed.

Saturday, November 29

Spent the night in this Shangri-la noted in yesterday's entry and, as a compromise, arose at the ungodly hour of 4:30 A.M. and walked to an alternate site for viewing the sunrise. They sky was absolutely clear, a very unusual phenomenon here, or so they say. The scenery to and from the viewing site is more than spectacular but, as sunrises go, I've seen just as fine from the breakfast table at Glynnspring. After a bit more viewing and photography, we summoned our daredevil jeep driver and descended the several seemingly endless miles to the little village where we had left the car.

It took a little time to round up the driver to our car and to check the car out so there was time to do some more viewing.

I talked to some Japanese tourists, one of whom spoke excellent English. More interesting was watching and trying to communicate with some of the desperately poor villagers who try to eke a living from the sides of these mountains. Terraces of only six to eight feet wide with various vegetables in between. It's too high and cold here for rice. My conclusion is that existence is hard on men and hell on women, but they know no other.

We then traveled down the fifteen or twenty miles of wonderful scenery and terrifying road.

From there on the day was anti-climactic. Traveled at a more or less leisurely pace on fairly passable roads to the large city of Surabaya. There, for a variety of reasons, we changed our plans: the first, the climate of this place is atrocious—100 degrees and one hundred percent humidity — and the city is filthy and odiferous. Our plan had been to dismiss Felix and return either by boat or train to Jakarta but the soonest we could get a boat was not for several days. So that was out and the next available train was not to leave until the next afternoon. We thus made the decision to retain Felix and make a two and a half day return through the center of this island of Java. And so we have returned some one hundred miles and are now bivouacked in a slightly crummy hotel in the very crummy oil town of Cepu. I am now trying to call John to tell him of our change of schedule. Will have a bite to eat and then lay this powerful frame to rest. Good night!

Sunday, November 29

Probably a short entry today as most of the day was spent in travel, and a good deal of that in the rain. Arose about 7:00 and had the usual breakfast that goes with the room in these parts; toast (made from slightly stale bread), juice, coffee, and jam. And we're ready to take off for John's, a two-day trip. But no Felix! Our "trusty" guide was making use of what they call rubber time here. When he finally did arrive, cheerful as a canary, he said "Ready so soon? I thought you said ten o'clock!"

We then did take a rather leisurely drive through a beautiful teak forest, a state monopoly, and stopped to watch the very very primitive but selective logging operations. Then the rains came and the rest of the day was spent looking out the car window at the countryside. Interesting but unremarkable, one downpour after another. Darkness fell and I do mean fell; there's practically no twilight in these climes: it's daylight to darkness with little in between, especially in such weather as today.

We groped our way into, what was to me, an unknown town of unknown location and found lodgings. The long and short of it is that we will not arrive at John's tomorrow, in part because of the weather.

Will now try to call John to that affect. My worthy Carp and honest (?) Felix have gone out to eat. I'm sitting here in the "lobby" watching a bugger who speaks about ten words of English try to make telephone connections with Jakarta. He is now conferring with three or four aides or superiors about the call. In all probability he will soon bow and say, "So sorry, but the connection is not well tonight." But then, I'm getting used to the ways of the mysterious East. Incidentally, this Felix of ours is one of the most enigmatic and fascinating persons I have ever had contact with and, I believe worthy of a small monograph which I shall pen in due time. My bevy of telephone experts have, I believe, given up. But I shall try again. And soon to bed.

PS: A couple of German tourists just came in seem to be eager to engage in conversation. In English, I hope. And so it shall be done.

Monday, November 30

Arose, shaved and showered in semi-cold water. Had the breakfast that goes with the room and, wonder of wonders, Felix showed up on time. As I think I mentioned before, we had rearranged our schedule so as to return to Jakarta late this evening. But on re-survey found that it would be impossible. Tried futilely to call John to that effect. But this morning we went to the telephone office and made contact. We then took off through the usual interesting and vivid countryside in a generally westerly direction. It was interesting, but after so long, one rice paddy gets to look like another rice paddy. Then we crossed and recrossed the central mountainous spine of this island. Breathtaking it was. Fortunately we chanced upon a village that was having its annual fete. Everybody in weird costumes, playing weird music on weird instruments. Felix explained that the "musicians" expected a small contribution, which we gladly gave. Carp as usual filmed it all.

Driving these narrow roads is an experience like no other. I think that these wily Orientals have found a way to avoid building institutions for the insane: every time they have an absolutely certifiably mad man on their hands they give him a job as a bus driver! As dusk approached, the rain, as usual, came down in torrents. Upon arriving at the town scheduled as our night stop our honest (?) Felix professed that he could find no lodgings. The reason being that Felix had every intention of detouring us to his hometown for the night. And so here we are, some fifty miles further from Jakarta than we should have been. But one can't but admire the way the damned bugger can manipulate. So we are now in a rather fancy hotel in Bandung and Felix is in the bosom of his family. Will now go down and walk the streets for a while to get the kinks out of my legs. And then will go to bed...

Tuesday, December 1

Today is supposed to be the last leg of an extended tour of Java with an ETA at John's about 3:00 P.M. But with our worthy guide Felix one never knows. We leave the city of Bandung (2.5 million population) on the only really modern road I've seen in Indonesia: about fifteen miles of four-lane road equal to any seen in the United States, practically all built with hand labor. A few heavy machines were used, but very few. Looking at it from all angles this "inefficiency" is really efficient. Were it done "our" way the requisite machine manufacturer would have created thirty to forty thousand high-paying jobs in Japan, the United States or Germany and used up untold millions of scarce foreign currency, and eliminated jobs for some millions untrained Indonesians, for whom there would be no other occupation. One must look at such things through the eyes of the local population.

At any rate, our smooth, fast track soon came to an end and back it was to the narrow mountainous "main" road to Jakarta.

Unfortunately the most scenic part was obscured by fog and rain. From what we could see, however, this area must be absolutely breathtaking. All arable land in this area is covered with tea, a labor-intensive crop that employs, at subsistence wages (even by the standards of this country) some millions of workers, mostly women.

After breaking out of fog at lower altitude we were again in rice country. Beautiful landscape but by now old hat to us. The villages, each containing some 10,000 to 20,000 souls, seemed to be wholly engaged in some traditional and hereditary occupation. One such was rope-making. All, and I mean "all" of this village, seemed to be rope-making. All done by hand, using nothing but waste from textile and plastic mills. Very serviceable rope of all sizes and colors. We spent an hour or so here viewing and asking questions and, as usual, Carp filmed the whole procedure.

Two or more stops worthy of note were made: One was a gong and drum and wooden musical instruments factory. All work was done in exactly the same manner as was employed prior to

117

Felix

Felix, our guide on a two-week tour of back country Java is, I think, the most enigmatic man in this enigmatic land, and therefore worthy of a small monograph.

First a bit about his background: Like all things about this chameleon-like character, one can never be sure, but as near as I can make out he is by ancestry one-quarter Dutch and three-quarters Javanese. His family seems to have been of the upper middleclass or minor rich and of the family he was the charming black sheep.

Trying to analyze such a character would have driven old Sigmund Freud nuts, and to describe him would have been too much for Willie Shakespeare, so I shall not presume to be their better.

As to his education, it seems to have been broad but not deep. He attended several of the better schools in his home city of Bandung but left each, either to the great relief, or at the request, of the faculty. Somewhere along the line he acquired fluency in English, Dutch and German. He married into a rich Chinese-Indonesian family. His wife is a well-known M.D. in his city. Then to the horror of all he decided to become a tour guide. This was due to his incurable curiosity as to all things geographical and humanistic. As to religion, he professes to be a Christian, but is equally at home with the holy men of Islam, Buddha, Hindu and the witch doctors of the old animists. If he has any belief, I think it leans towards the latter. This gives him a great advantage in his work, as he can sweettalk and bribe these holy men and knows the proper bribe to slip these guardians of virtue. He did in this manner get us into places and sites that none but true and pious pilgrims had ever trod, always in the guise of recent and enthusiastic converts of their faith.

There is a sort of sliding scale to these bribes. The holier the keeper of the shrine the bigger the bribe, but all in all, it is relatively small. These fakirs, mullahs or what have you could take a lesson from American TV preachers and learn to steal on a truly grand scale.

Among other attributes to admire in Felix is that he is also a thief, I think, but that is not all bad, as he probably steals no more than is readily available. He is also an admirable liar, inasmuch as he only lies when convenient. Admirable traits, don't you think? Above all, Felix is the consummate actor. He can get his clients into the most private of homes or most public of forums with his amazing aplomb. Another endearing trait is that he is a most incorrigible tom cat with a camp wife near each of his planned bivouacs. To sum up I would say that our Felix is a most efficient and lovable rogue, but a rogue still.

the advent of Christ. Most edifying but beyond the power of this poor pen to describe. Carp has it all on film. Number two was the famed botanical gardens of Bogor, located about an hour south of Jakarta. This site is a famous center for studies for botanists world wide, but I will not attempt to describe it.

Then an easy trip to John's, arriving there at about 5:30 P.M. with John pulling in a few minutes later. After effusive greetings, a badly needed shower, and a change of clothes (I had been out of clean clothes for some three days) we settled up with our honest (?) Felix and bid him a fond adieu.

John then announced that we were invited to a gala reception and farewell party for some large wig at the Australian embassy. The party was in itself most impressive and the guest list even more so. There were a whole passel of Indonesian cabinet ministers, a larger group of social climbing phonies—all important in their own way—and, so far as Carp was concerned, a real live sultan, a greasy fat bore of great wealth. To cap it all off there were several tables groaning under the weight of all manner of delectable food and, continuously circulating among the milling guests, were a bevy of little fellows dressed in white and wearing turbans bearing trays of conversations makers: wine, brandy, beer etc. I was impressed and I think Carp even more so. I noticed him in animated conversation with our worthy host and slapping the back of the sultan. As was mentioned before, the man has a healthy curiosity, but I fear his sense of protocol is not sufficiently developed.

From thence back to our digs at John's where I am about to lay this powerful frame down to sleep of the just. Tomorrow will be dedicated to rest, rest and more rest.

This day of rest was done with great enthusiasm. Arose late to be immediately attacked by some invisible servant with a tray of coffee, tea, juice and fruit. After thanking the invisible in a silent manner, we did partake. Then, after the usual ablution, went to John's house. I've probably failed to describe his ménage: his office, work place and guest house, where we are domiciled, is three doors from his home, where we were served a full breakfast.

Carp, having read one of the slogans pasted everywhere "Let us waste nothing," did his duty. He consumed his breakfast and mine, too. Carp then went off with John's car and driver to investigate the possibility, practicality, and cost of a side trip to Singapore and Malaysia. I then spent the day as planned, with rest, refit and recuperation. Carp, according to his wishes, was taken to the city center and left to his own devices. He made arrangements for everything and returned home in a three-wheel vehicle pedaled by a muscular fellow, and Carp sitting up front looking like a Buddha with indigestion and a cat that had just devoured a canary. An excellent dinner at John's, and then to bed...

Arose at a reasonable hour and after the usual morning's ritual we, with John's driver, Eko, at the wheel, departed for downtown Jakarta where we "finalized" the purchase of air tickets to Singapore. From thence our itinerary is indefinite: probably Malaysia, maybe Sumatra... It is all in the hands of Allah. Then to the National Museum of Indonesia, a most interesting and educational place, but I fear ill arranged and infested with "volunteer" guides who don't know a damned thing. Then back "home" and the usual excellent dinner. Some conversation with a couple of French linguists who are studying here, a few well deserved brandies, and then to the land of happy dreams.

Friday, December 4

Having purchased tickets to Singapore for 9:30 A.M. we were deposited by John's driver at the Jakarta airport for a flight to Singapore. The flight was on time but from there on the rest of the day was disappointing. Firstly we were supposed to fly over or near the famed volcano of Krakatoa, which is now in eruption. We did, but nothing but clouds above, below, to the right, and to the left. Allah is not to be questioned.

Having the well wishes of the gods, we arrived at Singapore. Having in my youth followed the rise, and later, the fall of the British Empire, I expected more of the Kiplingesque here, but, unfortunately, a reasonably incorrupt government has been in control for some time and unwisely, in my opinion, "modernized" the place. The whole island is incredibly clean. Lodgings are exorbitant. Food is reasonable, and public transportation is unbelievably cheap. The whole place has an air of phoniness. We leave in the morning. Shall now bathe and shave—probably with cold water—and will then go to bed.

Saturday, December 5

Having been in Singapore but a short day and I, being disappointed with the place, did decide to head for more exotic areas. Got a bus ticket to Kuala Lumpur, capital of Malaysia. But another word or two about Singapore: In spite of its too quick modernization and thoughtless ignoring of its historical past, the government and population as a whole must be admired for the way they have proved since independence that colonialism was not any blessing to our "little brown brothers." They are, I believe, an example to the "emerging nations." Very properous, indeed, compared to Indonesia and what we've seen so far of Malaysia.

Most of the day was taken up by a six-hour bus ride through southern Malaysia to this city. All day was cloudy and a good part of it rainy, so not a good time for viewing or tasting the culture. Even so, some things are obvious. First and foremost, compared to Indonesia, it was not thought worth plundering by European powers or missionaries — at least until the bicycle craze of the 1880s and 90s created an insatiable demand for rubber. This I suppose is due to the difference in soil and terrain and the fact that up to a century or two ago this area was the home of scattered aboriginal tribes, and so had a small population base from which to grow. It was this, along with the fact that the soil and climate of these parts are perfect for rubber cultivation and that cheap (slave or indentured) labor was available, which caused the greedy and pious Dutch and English to catch the Brazilian rubber barons in swimming and ran off with their clothes.

At present, with the price of natural rubber being comparatively low due to the inereased use of synthetic materials, great areas of the vast colonial rubber plantations are being converted to oil palm —not coconut— from which palm oil is extracted and used to manufacture margarine and hundreds of other things. But I have seen it through a bus window and am ill prepared to write a paper on the subject.

Most of the lore of rubber and palm oil put to paper here was provided by a retired planter with whom I had several beers in the very reasonably priced bar in this extremely reasonably priced hotel. Prices here seem to be less than half those of Singapore.

I forgot to mention that the great tin mines north of here are now all closed due to the low price of tin, once again because of an increased use of alternative synthetic materials and cheaper tin from the mines of Brazil and Bolivia.

Having penned this learned paper I am in need of well earned rest and will now consign myself to the arms of Morpheus and sleep the sleep of the just.

Sunday, December 6

Awoke—Thanks be to Allah!—and being completely at loose ends in this large city in a completely strange land, decided on free-lance adventure for the day. Fortunately our omnipresent bellboy, who spoke excellent English, informed us he had a brother who could be "begged" to accompany us on a public transportation tour of the area. The brother was summoned and did agree to accompany us for the day for the princely sum of ten ringgits, or about US$ 2.50. The fellow proved to be a jewel.

First we rode around this very clean and apparently prosperous city on city buses. I believe that public surface transport in these parts is ridiculously inexpensive. Among other places, the piece de resistance was a tour of the largest mosque outside of Istanbul in the Moslem world. It was breathtaking. It was built in the 1960s at a cost of almost US$ 100 million. With Islam being the "state" religion of Malaysia, all taxpayers contributed. Come to think of it, that sum would be about one half the cost of one U.S. aircraft carrier. Further, the building will last one hundred times longer and will probably contribute a devil of a lot more to the peace of mankind, thanks be to Allah.

Our jolly little gnome of a guide, being a devout follower of Islam, was a perfect companion. We did have a leisurely tour of this vast edifice, barefoot of course, as is the wont.

No cameras are allowed in the interior but Carp was free to tape the grounds and exterior, which he did, to excess, I think. The delicacy and airiness of the whole compound is such a contrast to the immense and somehow gloomy cathedrals of Europe that it gives one to think.

After this spiritual experience we, at the suggestion of our gnome, took the city bus (at 40 cents each) to the old tin, rubber, and spice port city of Klang some twenty kilometers away. There we were fortunate enough to get passage on a ferry through the storied straits of Malacca, sites of battles and piracy from the time since the minds of men runneth to the contrary.

The ferry ride was an adventure in itself. The vessel was jammed to the gunwales with every form of humanity, produce—from coconuts to rather ripe fish—and two half-lost Americans.

About two hours later we arrived at a place called Crab Island, called so with good reason: It is a settlement of some 10,000 souls completely built on piling or stilts about eight feet above "ground" but at extremely high tide the whole place is above water.

The population is almost all ethnic Chinese and speak a Chinese dialect. Their total life and occupation is catching excellent crab and shrimp. Our very knowledgeable little guide knew nothing of the language, but with sign language and motions got along very well. Had an excellent meal of—What else?—crab, rice, and tea. We then caught another ferry of the same type back to the mainland and, as the hour was growing late, returned to our hotel. After mutual protestations of affection we did pay off our guide and, by this time, friend. We tipped him two packs of cigarettes (37 cents each) and then, due to our very close proximity to packed humanity and rancid fish, took a much needed bath. Now will write a letter to Mother, and then to bed...

Monday, December 7

Awoke, did the usual ablution, spent about an hour trying to rouse my crew, Carp. He last night did fall among evil companions at a place called the Hard Rock Cafe. It seems that these establishments are the "in" thing with the younger crowd and he wanted to get T-shirts for his daughters. At any rate it seems he fell in with a pair of raucous Aussies and was suffering from an old tropical disease: a horrendous hangover. After giving him verbal chastisement, I managed to get him fairly mobile. Went to breakfast; coffee for me and juice, fruit, toast, three eggs, and bacon for my patient. His strength was restored. It seems that the sight of a menu is a cure-all for his illnesses, real or imagined. Then we met our little interpreter of yesterday and sallied forth on another guided tour. Compared to yesterday's excursion, the day was anti-climactic, but still edifying. Visited another mosque and the Chinese quarter. (It seems that all these smaller Asian nations have a large and very influential population of ethnic Chinese.) After that, the national museum and, last but not least, the government quarter, both colonial and post colonial. Very instructional, from an historical angle. Then returned to our hotel and after parting from our little interpreter with still more professions of mutual esteem, returned to our room where I am writing this.

I think that after shaving etc. I shall go to one of the numerous small native restaurants down the street and dine. The food is inexpensive and nourishing, though completely mysterious, at least to me. Will leave my crew to snore, roll and groan to his heart's content as we must leave in the morning on a bone cracking bus for Singapore, then to Jakarta, and John's. I have no worry about Carp's calorie intake, as during our day he did stop at several eateries and, as a result, he is on the outside of at least a whole chicken, great gobs of rice, sweet and sour pork, and God knows what other kinds of Oriental cookery.

Have returned from the safari mentioned above and find my crew still suffering, snoring and rolling, but such are the wages of sin.

Having some time on my hands and nothing to read, I shall pen my impressions of this new nation called Malaysia, although, God knows, this log already grows overlong.

Firstly, the contrast between here and Indonesia is beyond belief. The people here seem to be almost wealthy, which is probably due to several facts. First is the county's relatively sparse population, which is less than one tenth that of Indonesia. Following that is the country's more abundant natural resources (at least in per capita terms), including oil, rubber, tin, tea, and palm oil. Also, and probably more important, is their colonial past. The Dutch in Indonesia were more oppressive than were the British in Malaysia and regarded any native of that land who could read as a threat to the regim. As a result, very few were educated.

The British colonial model, meanwhile, depended on the existence of a well-trained corps of "civil servants" who, when independence approached, were capable of taking the reigns of their new nation. Then too, when the British saw the writing on the wall, that the end of colonialism was night, they left the country with comparative dignity and good will. The Dutch, on the other hand, had to be forced out of Indonesia through a lengthy, costly, and bloody revolutionary war, the aftermath of which was that no other force except the military was in a position to forge a new nation. And now, after almost fifty years of Indonesian independence, the "generals" are still running the country! (From what I've seen, it seems that the structural organization in the Indonesian army calls for one general for each private soldier. But enough of this...)

Just one more word: Kuala Lumpur, the capital of Malaysia, is the cleanest city of its size (1.8 million) that I have ever seen.

I will now take the pulse of my sleeping, suffering, and overfed crew. And then to bed...

Tuesday, December 8

Awoke refreshed and after breakfast etc. did catch a semi-tour bus from the city of Kuala Lumpur to the old spice city of Malacca, which was fought over and changed hands numerous times through numerous centuries. First the Hindus, then the Muslims, then the Portuguese, then the Dutch, then the English, then the Japanese (in World War II), then the English again, and then freedom, involving several years of internecine war until finally emergings as a fairly stable and prosperous place, perhaps with many anomalies left over from centuries of subjugation but fairly well governed. From Kuala Lumpur there is little to see but endless miles of rubber and oil palm plantations. The city of Malacca is itself a living museum of the ebb and flow of invasions and subjugations. No great monument to be found there but the place itself is a sort of monument.

128

Towards evening we caught a public bus and arrived at Singapore in the dark and pouring rain. Were lucky to find a very cheap lodging place across from the bus station. Got a bite to eat in a nearby (real) Chinese restaurant and am now to lay this weary form to rest.

After sleeping the sleep of the just, or just sleeping, surveyed our hostelry and although the room was most satisfactory, the surroundings appeared, in the light of day, most dismal. The rest of the building seemed to be occupied by a bunch of odiferous "hippies," (both American and Europeans), hordes of cockroaches and it seemed that a large and healthy rat stood guard at every nook and cranny. Managers appeared to be part of a most evil and dangerous den of thieves. All in all one would not rate it a five-star place. But what the devil, we came here to sleep and sleep we did. Breakfast in this part of the world is part of the rent but Carp, being a closet hypochondriac, decided he wasn't hungry. I, however, being of a curious turn of mind, joined my fellow rabble at the festive board for excellent coffee, excellent jam, mediocre fruit, and moldy toast-pieces, which were tossed to the ever-present rats.

We then went to the airline office to reconfirm our tickets back to Jakarta and found that they had arbitrarily changed our departure time from 9:30 this evening to 1:30 this afternoon. It was okay with me but, at the same time, the offhand way things are done here irritated me—plus John expected to meet us at the Jakarta airport around midnight. So a dash to the airport by city bus—It is unbelievable how efficient and inexpensive that type of transportation is here—then back to Jakarta, arriving at about

3:00 P.M. Called John but to no avail; he along with car and driver were gone on business and wouldn't be back until later. So had to take a cab and arrived here at 5:00 P.M.

One word about the plane ride: disaster! It was a disaster. By chance I was assigned the worst seat on an extremely crowded plane and my neighbors on all sides consisted of a very raucous soccer team, coach, and trainer. Apparently they had celebrated a victory over Thailand by consuming vast quantities of garlic, durian (stinky fruit), and ripe fish heads just before boarding. Now I have nothing against garlic, but in moderation and at first-hand. As I was squeezed, jostled and probably sat upon by this group of jubilant athletes, who evinced their joy of victory with loud and numerous burps, the two-hour trip was, to say the least, interesting. Arrived at Jakarta unscathed but smelling of the sewers. Then to John's for a long and thorough shower, a leisurely dinner, some conversation, some planning for the morrow, then to sleep, perchance to dream of garlic and soccer players.

Thursday, December 10

Arose and as usual here there was a discreet knock on the door and a semi-visible servant appeared with coffee and fruit. Then up to John's house three doors away and had the usual breakfast, or at least Carp did (of toast, eggs, jam, fruit juice, fruit, and coffee) and then to the day's adventures. I say adventures because it mainly consisted of getting a much needed haircut at Rudy Hadisuwarno Salon, one of the top salons in the city where Wim, John's friend, is the manager and chief stylist. This Wim is the same Wim who had spent a holiday at Glynnspring and therefore felt constrained to give us the full treatment, at no cost to us! Cast your bread upon the waters etc.

This was not a haircut; it was a major operation. First one is seated in a half-chair, half-bathed and given a most thorough shampoo. At the same time a person is massaging ones arms and giving a manicure. After the shampoo one is moved to another room, placed in a different type of chair. Some preparation is placed on your hair and a most pleasant massage of head, neck, and shoulders ensues. Then another shampoo and one is ready for the haircut, or styling, which Wim did perform in a most deft manner. I came out feeling ten years younger and looking ten days younger.

Did then return to John's to sort out things and repack prior to leaving with John for Bali for four days—9:00 A.M. tomorrow—and from thence the long flight back to U.S.A. and home before Christmas.

Tonight John is having a small farewell party for us, ten or twelve friends. Will now return to packing and will do today's journal post party.

Returned after a very convivial dinner and conversation. About a dozen guests, all of the most cosmopolitan types. The same crew would be equally at home in Paris, London or Timbuktu. And now to bed...

Friday, December 11

Arose about 7:00, double-checked our packing, had the usual breakfast (or rather "breakfasts"), then embarked by car for the airport through the damnedest traffic jam you ever did see, with Wim at the wheel and John as the guide and guardian angel to take our flight to Bali. In fact, the first leg of the long journey home. Although I am enjoying myself immensely I find myself longing a bit for the hills of home.

Arrived in Bali about two o'clock and checked into a lovely place on the beach, partially owned by Toenggoel Siagian, a friend (and former professor) of John's. I don't know how much we have to pay, but not much, I think, as this same friend was at dinner last night and I overheard John and him discussing some cozy arrangement in three different languages.

Settled in, cleaned up and rested till nightfall, then out to eat at a "Mexican" restaurant operated by an expatriate family from Tibet. I think the meal was minced yak meat, black rice and great gobs of chili peppers. In short, not good at all. Then to the house of Dan Scherer, the soon-to-be former son-in-law of Virginia Johnson, John's volunteer secretary. Dan hailed some twenty years ago from the state of Washington and is now engaged in importing specialty foods to supply all the posh hotels here and, it seems to me, is prospering greatly. We had numerous cocktails and good conversation. Then by his car home and then to bed...

Saturday, December 12

Having been a bit late in arriving "home", and having been well plied with excellent and various fine wines, liqueur, cigars, food and scintillating conversation, and having no particular reason to greet the rising sun, we did sleep late, the latest of the whole trip, arising about 8:30.

After the usual rigmarole, had a light breakfast at a little open-air restaurant built on the high tide line of this sprawling cottage-type hotel complex. One reason that we were in no hurry was that John had contracted for a rental car and it would not be here till noon. Sitting in this place on a beautiful beach in front of us, with time on hand, gave us, or me at least, a chance to study the strange species called "tourist" that infest, litter, and corrupt this pristine island. By and large, I think, they are the most obnoxious, arrogant, and ignorant group ever to be seen in one place. Mostly are of the "new rich" type and come to these highly advertised and over-priced resorts. They appear on the strand about 10:00 A.M., not to see but to be seen. The worst of the lot are the females, mostly early middle-aged misshapen bags dressed in dark glasses, a towel about their ample necks, and a "swim suit" that does a totally inadequate job of holding their sagging breasts, bulging backsides, and spindly white legs together. They then sit on the sand a bit, stroll around a bit trying to impress the other basking whales, dropping names such as "I told Lady Di," or "the Aga Khan called last night." After totally failing to impress anybody they return to their US$ 300 per night hotel room and, I suspect, spend the rest of the day in a beauty salon. But, I fear, to no avail. The male of this sub-species is not so evident. Presumably they never leave the air-conditioned comfort of their expensive digs, getting splotched on US$ 10 expense-account martinis and scheming as to how to replenish their ill-gotten gains with more thievery.

After the car did arrive we took off on an abbreviated tour—partly pleasure and partly business—the business part being John stopping at several bookstores and delivering books to one. Took pleasure in simply observing the beautiful countryside of the southern part of this island, trying to absorb a bit of the feeling of the Hindu-Balinese culture of this beautiful isle. Impossible in a short time, I fear. And visual treats, particularly the ancient and impressive Hindu temple of Tanah Lot that rises on a promontory on the coast and at high tide is cut off by the water. But we were there at low tide and could approach as far as religious norms allow to explore the place.

133

Then back to this place, and being travel worn and weary, I was ready for a long night's sleep. John, however, had a message to call someone, the result being that the three of us were invited to a dinner party at the home of a friend of John's. I, however, feeling weary and not at all hungry, declined.

John and Carp went. I, after bathing etc., felt fully recharged and regretted having declined the invitation. But, too late. I walked to a nearby restaurant and pub and had a beer and conversed with a very cultured old Chinese man and am now back here completing this day's journal. Whether sleep descends on me is now in the hands of Allah.

Saturday, December 13

Arose a bit later than planned, probably due to the fact that our shades were fully closed. I, being the first one up and about, showered, shaved, and then awoke my two sleeping beauties. Neither had nearly as much sleep as I. Then I, and I alone, went across the way to the aforementioned small restaurant for a "Continental" of toast, jam, coffee and fruit. Then returned to find my two companions up and about and went in search of an English-language newspaper. But no luck.

Returned and found John and Carp bright-eyed and bushy-tailed and almost ready to go. And go we did. Checked out of the hotel to start on a partly-planned and partly ad-lib tour of central and north Bali. That part of the island is much more mountainous than the south and of great natural beauty. Besides observing the natural beauty of the mountains and agriculture, we did visit, among other places, Besakih, the site of the largest and oldest complex of Hindu temples outside of India. Incidentally, the people of Bali must be complete temple nuts, as every town, no matter how small, has a main temple. In addition, there are small temples scattered all over the place. But back to our big one: it was very old, mystifying, and so blasted ugly that it is almost pretty. We spent about two and a half hours there and were most impressed. I failed to mention that it was built or at least started to be built in the seventh century. And in spite of numerous earthquakes and the fact that about a fourth of it was completely obliterated by a volcanic eruption in 1967, it has withstood the heavy hand of time remarkably well. The reason for its location is that it is on the side of Mount Batur, the holy or "mother" mountain of Bali. It was this mother that blew her top and buried part of it. But such is the will of the Almighty, or spirits, or whatever it is that we Hindus worship.

Upon leaving there, the hour having grown later than we realized, and the evening downpour about due, we wended our way down the mountain through steep and narrow valleys to the sea and found lodging in Candidasa, a small city on the eastern coast of the island. Being rather weary, we had a quick, light dinner and then to bed...

Monday, December 14

I awoke this A.M. a bit later than usual, about 7:00, because the other two tend to sleep late in the morning. And as the beach and surf were just outside, I did for the second time since being here, go swimming in the Pacific Ocean or an arm thereof. Very nice. Returned to find my two companions trying to come out of their nightly coma, helped them along a bit, and after the usual continental breakfast, we were ready to embark on our second-to-last day of adventure and discovery in these strange lands. As much as I have enjoyed, and am still enjoying, this wonderful

TOURISTS

While it ill fits me to give an in-depth appraisal of this strange breed of dog called "tourist," based on six weeks of intensive travel it is impossible not to have formed some prejudices and conclusions. So, right or wrong, I shall put them to paper. After, but not until after I complete this learned tome, I shall compare my thoughts with several professional guides and numerous long-term expatriates and see if their evaluations coincide with mine.

Firstly these foreign visitors must be cross indexed in several ways. The first is by nationality. The second is by goup size: large organized tour groups, small groups, or single tourists (such as we, Carp and I). The third kind of tourist comprises the professional wanderer, the religious nut in search of the "truth" (most of whom are as phony as a three-dollar bill), and the just plain bum who thinks the world owes him a living.

As to tour "groups," by nationality, by far the most numerous are Dutch, next the Germans, then Japanese followed by Australians. A group, as I define the meaning here, consists of five or more persons who are following a pre-planned and inflexible schedule, who travel with a guide, and, quite apparently, a preconceived idea as to how they should "do" this vast land in six days, twenty-two hours and thirteen minutes. (In fact, such docile cattle would absorb no real insight into the mysteries of this vast and diverse land in a lifetime.)

I failed to mention the dregs of the "tourists." Shall categorize them and then let them be reincarnated as leeches, which they deserve. These are the "fact-finding groups," American congressmen and their retinue—minor European politicos, African and Asian nabobs who spend a few days here (in an alcoholic haze) are given a tin medal of some sort, run up astronomical bills at the Hyatt or Hilton, all financed by their over-burdened taxpayers at home, then depart on the next leg of their journey of thievery. Enough said of this type, but in the eyes of minor functionaries, tradesmen, and beggars, they are to be picked and loathed. No more will be said of them.

Back to the tour groups—the Dutch. In spite of their education and experience they regard this vast land as their rightful heritage temporarily in the hands of their minions. They could not be more wrong. The locals, from tour guides, lowest of the peasants, to government dignitaries, politely accept them, cater to them, take their money, and loathe them.

The Germans tend to run in larger groups, stay closer together, make no effort to communicate with the local populace. Although a majority of them can speak some, and in many cases excellent, English one must make the approach. After breaking the ice one finds individuals who are most compatible, friendly and cultured. And they like cold beer. But once the conversation and the beer have been exhausted they go back to their flock .... together.

The Japanese, they also tend to have a herding in-stinct and I get the feeling they are detested by both Indonesians and Malaysians, probably in memory of their double crossing and then plundering them dur-ing World War II.

trip, I find myself thinking more often of the rice paddies, coconut groves, and rubber plantations of Wisconsin. At any rate, our first objective was a very active volcano, Mount Batur, whose prehistoric eruption must have been one of the greatest explosions of all times, leaving as it did, a crater or caldera about twenty one miles wide and God knows how deep. Since then, a whole new mountain has grown up inside, which, in 1917, experienced a major eruption, killing many thousands of people. Nonetheless intensive agriculture still goes on within this vast natural theater, and there still are numerous jets of acrid steam emitted at various places. The population here, like the peasant Italian grape-growers on the sides of Etna and Vesuvius, seem to be totally fatalistic. "If it blows, it blows." But come to think of it, all of mankind is figuratively "sitting on a volcano."

After an abbreviated tour of the volcano, we stopped and found quarters for the night in Ubud, an "arty" town where John has several "arty" and expatriate friends whom he wants to call or call on. Will thus finish this what adventures the day holds. In this area, John seems to have contact with, or is intimately acquainted with, most of the local intelligentsia and the educated expatriates, some of whom I find to be a little too much.

I, being a good soul, returned to quarters and read both the Koran and the bible religiously.... In what other way could I read them? Now, being full of wisdom, did I consign my night to the arms of Allah.

December 15

Arose before my companions, as usual, and went forth to find the numerous frogs who serenaded us through the dark and rainy night. Fortunately a young lady or girl of some fifteen summers who "works" here showed me their lair. During the sunlight hours they snooze under immense lily pads. I learned that the male of the species conducts the horrendous concert of the night, but is comparatively small, about the size of a coconut. The female, from which the famous Balinese frog legs come, are about the size of a poodle, and a damned sight prettier and tastier.

Having received my degree as Dr. of Froggery, I returned to the compound of domicile. Then, with John as guide, went forth to do a little shopping. For me, some little thing for my long-suffering spouse and her deserving kinder. Mission accomplished, with John's advice, language and long-time acquaintance with the haggling system of these parts.

Poor Carp, however, in his wisdom, for some strange reason thinks he can out-haggle the hagglers. As a result he's accumulated the most God-awful collection you ever did see, among them two blow guns, some fifteen or twenty rings, great quantities of earrings and, I think, a gross of T-shirts. I don't care, but I have to help carry them home.

The hour grows late and tomorrow is take-off time for home, so will go to bed.

December 16

Slept as long as possible this morning (as we have, I think, twenty-two hours of flight ahead of us), breakfasted, packed, and then John took us out to the airport—which is when the frustration started! On checking in for our flight we were informed that it would be "slightly" delayed. The plane was supposed to leave at one o'clock but, after a bit, it was announced that due to technical problems the flight would not leave until nine o'clock P.M.! So all the passengers were loaded in minibuses and transported to a fancy hotel and given rooms (which to me was superfluous as I can't sleep in the daytime anyway) as well as two meal tickets, for lunch and dinner. We were informed that the busses would pick us up at 8:15, the result was that instead of saying good-bye to John at the airport we arranged to meet in the hotel lobby towards evening, which we did, and, after affectionate farewells were made, we duly arrived at the airport. Checked through immigration and waited for the "nine o'clock" plane, and waited and waited and waited. Just before midnight we took off. We are now in the air between Bali and our first fueling stop, Biak, a minor port in a major ocean. The result of all this is that it might mess up our connections between Los Angeles and San Francisco. Did send a message to Mary. This night will I will not sleep.

December 17

Not really much to write about this day? The reason for the question mark is that sometime between here and Los Angeles we shall cross the international date line, picking up the day that we "lost" while flying west, but cross about eight time zones, losing an hour each. I will not be sure of either the day or hour, and won't be for a while. Anyway, landed at Biak for fuel, but I for one did not leave the plane, as it was still rather dark and there's really nothing there but an old World War II bomber strip. Think I failed to mention that it was a much larger plane on the way over, a 747, seating almost four hundred and a crew of at least twenty-five. At any rate, we flew on for the next twenty hours, except for a forty-five minute refuel stop, and finally arrived at Los Angeles airport.

Due to our lengthy delay in Bali, our connecting flight to San Francisco was messed up. Garuda, our airline, was supposed to have notified Mary of the change but failed to do so. I tried to call Mary from Los Angeles but could get nothing but an answering machine. Finally, after about a two-hour wait did get a flight to San Francisco and had to take an airport shuttle bus to Mary's. She, expecting us the previous evening, had gone to the airport to no avail. Did arrive at Mary's to find that both she and Rick had left at 6:00 A.M. for one of their seminars and wouldn't return until 6:00 P.M. But no worry, we had no intention of doing anything but going to bed and catching up on sleep—thirty hours and ten time zones plus jet lag—and so we did.

A new December 17

Slept for several hours and, upon arising, did declare it a new day, and spent the rest of the afternoon repacking, in preparation for leaving here as early as possible in the morning for the long drive home. Called my dear wife to announce our arrival back on the mainland. Among other things, she told was that she had fallen on the ice and "sort of" hurt her leg. She said it wasn't much, but it worries me some.

We did a considerable batch of washing, as we both were getting very low on everyday clothes. Failed to mention that we had constant help from little Kate during our packing. Mary and Rick arrived as expected and, after effusive greetings, they took us out to dinner. Upon returning, had some conversation about our soon-to-be-completed trip, and soon to bed in preparation for leaving early in the morn. Will now call this a complete day.

Arose early, as planned, and after fond farewells took off through the hellish traffic of San Francisco, with Carp at the wheel. I must say he's an excellent driver and from his ten years of cross-country truck driving he seems to be well acquainted with all the streets and roads in the land. Negotiated the traffic very well past Sacramento but at that time both the roads through the Sierra Nevada Mountains and the weather turned ugly and slowed us up somewhat. Even so, we made better progress than I had expected. I had been hoping to arrive home in four days, partly because of worry about Mother's leg, and partly because of the fact that Christmas will soon be upon us, and I would like to have a few days at home before going away for Christmas. It started to grow dark early and the roads got worse—icy—so we stopped a little sooner than intended, in Elko, Nevada. There's about a foot of snow on the ground. The temperature is supposed to be below zero in the morning. Ye Gods! To think that two days ago we were just south of the equator in ninety-degree weather! Will soon go out to get a bite to eat, and then to bed. If the weather and roads don't improve, I fear our e.t.a. in Cazenovia will be a day later than hoped.

December 19

Probably a short entry this day as the schedule called for nothing but driving, as we will have two very full days of that. Awoke in the town of Elko, Nevada, and heard a weather report to the effect that the coldest spot in the area was—Guess where?—in Elko, with a temperature of minus fifteen degrees. Though still in bed, the news made me shiver.

Sallied forth, had some coffee, and departed. Drove through snow-covered landscape: very scenic but nothing spectacular. Drove steadily for well over five hundred miles with Carp at the wheel doing the bulk of the driving. Arrived at a snow-covered Cheyenne, Wyoming, about nine o'clock. Drove somewhat farther than intended as we were just ahead of another storm and thought it well to stay that way. Found a room and quickly went to bed.

December 20

Arose about seven o'clock to be greeted by the sun rising in a beautiful clear sky, but a bitterly cold day. Drove through about fifty miles of low snow-covered mountains of Wyoming, then seemingly endless miles of flat and snow-covered Nebraska. The snow cover ceased west of Omaha, our object for the day. But as it was not yet dark we extended the day's trip to Des Moines, Iowa, leaving but an easy drive for the morrow, our last day of the trip. Should arrive at Glynnspring shortly past noon and hope to find the native in residence friendly. A light meal and early to bed.

December 21

The last day of our nine-week odyssey was an easy one—about three hundred miles of good, fairly-level, and dry roads. Nothing of note, really, between Des Moines, Iowa, and our home port, probably because through the years the terrain has become familiar—and as is said, familiarity breeds contempt. I would have no doubt that a native of Tibet would find this level and fertile land breathtaking, but such is the perversity of human nature, and also the reason that voyages of discovery, such as ours soon to be concluded, are launched.

Arrived at the home port of Glynnspring and found no one there. Mother had gone to the funeral of an old and valued neighbor, Loraine Mitchell.

The Captain then dismissed the whole crew—Carp—with our sturdy ship, a 1988 Plymouth, and bade him to return said ship on the morrow, after unloading his plunder accumulated from all sorts of street vendors and Hard Rock Cafes. A partial bill of lading would, I think, include seventy-nine T-shirts, thirty-seven "valuable" rings, twenty-three pairs of earrings and half a ton of memorabilia such as hotel receipts, unused post cards etc. I, the Captain, then eagerly awaited the return of my bride of some near fifty summers—come to think of it, winters too! You know, absence does make the heart grow fonder. Soon the long neglected bride returned and after mutual and sincere effusion of affection, prepared to settle down to domesticity. And will soon to bed —with Annie.

So ends this log. Had the notebook been thicker, the log would have been longer. Your old Captain does not presume to rank with my old friends Odysseus, Sinbad, Gulliver, or Marco Polo, but given sufficient years and funds, will try to gain on them.

My sealed orders were to determine the shape of the world. The final report is that all presumptions are in error. The blasted thing is nearly upside down. And so ends this log. *Adieu...*

John's Last (?) Hurrah

It is August of 1996 and this old man has decided to pack his bags and leave home—at least for a short while. As Mother can not be left alone, Kathleen has decided, of her own volition, to entertain Mother the time that I am away, thereby kindly permitting me to do a bit of aimless wandering, as is my wont.

The tentative plan is that after the upcoming weekend, one that is more than full of reunions—Mother's high school reunion near Richland Center, followed by a mad dash to Kathleen and Terry's in Eau Claire on Saturday, August 3, for a Schauf reunion in Menominee where all and sundry are supposed to gather on Sunday, the next day. (Of that particular assembled multitude I will probably know less than a dozen but will shake all hands and pat all fannies and be happier than hell.) Following attendance at these social affairs, I will return to Kathleen's where Mother will stay until yours truly, this reincarnation of Gulliver, Sinbad or, maybe even, Marco Polo, returns.

Before actually embarking I shall return home, Sunday evening. After my traveling companion, Mutzie Hanko, returns from a doctor's appointment on Monday, the next day, we shall take off in all directions at once, with no particular destination: maybe Las Vegas, maybe California, maybe Hub City. (Mutzie's

145

just finished a series of twenty-one radiation treatments following cancer surgery and so, I am sure, will have to be handled with care.) So, dear ones, after this extended introduction I propose to keep a skeletal log book of travels with Mutzie with the hope that it may be of interest to somebody.

Saturday, August 3, 1996

I did this day, as ordered, attend an Ithaca High School reunion for the classes of 1920-1940. For some reason there seemed to be a helluva lot of old people sitting around there, and I think half of them were dead. It also happened to be Mother's 60th class anniversary.

From thence, returned home, picked up some baggage and went to Kathleen's to help Terry's mother celebrate her birthday. On the whole it was a pleasant and fattening day.

Sunday, August 4, 1996

Attended the Schauf reunion in the city of Menominee, twenty-five miles north of Eau Claire. More food and most pleasant people. Did find, however, that the Irish were outnumbered 238 to one—all in all about even odds. Kathleen did come and, after sociabilities, took over the care and feeding of Mother for the next two weeks or so and sent me back home in a King-Lear manner, to wit old, mad, and alone. Did arrive back in Caz about 6:30 PM to disconcerting news: the Caz Reds had lost their first game of the season and, more worrisome, Mutzie had experienced a setback. But as his house was dark, I didn't stop in, and will call on him in the morning. Will now do a little packing and other preparations. After the various reunions and birthday parties, I shouldn't have to eat for a week. Will now to bed.

I did awake, thank the Lord, and busied myself with the household chores: making and consuming two cups of strong coffee. Then went to see Agnes and Jack, and then to Cazenovia to the post office to see about the mail and to await Mutzie's return from his thief of a doctor—<u>All</u> doctors are thieves, not just Mutzie's—hoping we would then mount our trusty Rosenante and ride off into the sunset.

But I was soon reminded the best laid plans of mice and men "gang oft aglae": Mutzie returned from the doctor's appointment with a long face: he had been informed that "things don't seem just right" and that he would have to go to Madison later in the week for further tests. So much for our plans!

What was to be done? What was I to do? A decision requires long and deep thought, and so it did—about fifteen seconds: I would go alone, by thumb. And, as a gesture to the long gone past, I would make it a sentimental journey, following, as nearly as possible, the course taken on my first youthful trip to the West. So, with the thinking done, I walked down to the mailbox and stuck out my thumb.

Things went rather well considering a late start and impromptu plans. My first ride was with Buffalo Conners who dropped me off at the new Richland Center High School. From there I next went to Viroqua with a construction worker. Next to La Crescent, Minnesota, and then to the city of Fairmont in that same state.

I could have gone further but thought it best to stop at little early—5:00 PM—as it looked stormy in the West. Further, after a rather hectic forenoon I do now feel the need of rest, refit, and map study.

147

As there are a couple of fast food joints across from this modest hostelry in which I stay I will patronize one and then go to bed.

Tuesday, August 6, 1996

Oh, but these are the worst of days and the best of days... I arose and ambled down to the interstate expecting an immediate ride to far places, but no such thing happened. This old man stood there for two hours and was just about to redo my sums as per an old man traveling when a little, timid-looking old man stopped and said that he was going "clear" to the next town—thirty-five miles hence.

At least the next town of Worthington, Minnesota was a change of scenery but there, too, I suffered yet another exercise in futility. Then, just as I was about to retire to my tent (as did Achilles in the Trojan Wars), a young man stopped and offered me a ride into the sunset.

The young man turned out to be a most enjoyable host; he was a first lieutenant in the cavalry (dismounted) and had recently been reassigned to Fort Lewis, Washington. His father and I were about the same age and we—his father and I—had both been stationed in England at the same time.

At any rate, my host said that he was going to Portland, Oregon, and I could go that far if I so wished. I did so wish and thus we proceeded together towards the setting sun.

The original plan had been to drive to Rapid City, South Dakota, and there to bivouac for the night. But alas and, probably, alack, there was a motorcycle rally being held in Sturgis, South Dakota, and every motel room within one hundred fifty miles had long since been taken. From an off-duty policeman we learned that there were 100,000—Yes, 100,000!—motorcycles registered, and probably 250,000 people.

So there we were, tossed on a sea of black-clad and goggled creatures from, I think, a number of different planets, leaving us no choice but to try and get some sleep in the van. That I couldn't hack so, in the end, I spent about six hours in an all-night restaurant, drinking coffee and talking to raucous characters from several planets.

My host, being a young cavalry officer used to bivouac, managed to greet the dawn fully refreshed.

Wednesday, August 7, 1996

Today we did travel, and travel, and travel: across the entire state of Montana and the panhandle of Idaho, stopping finally in Walla Walla, Washington, where I parted company with my benefactor of some thousand miles with profuse assurances of mutual esteem.

I am now ensconced in an over-priced motel where I shall shortly go to bed and catch up on some badly needed sleep.

Thursday, August 8, 1996

I awoke late to blistering hot daylight, breakfasted, and then hit the road. On the whole it was a frustrating day. Firstly, it was over 100 degrees and, secondly, while rides were numerous, they were very short.

My first ride was with a religious nut and her dog. She assured me that both of them were reborn something or another and implied that it was about time I took a whack at it. During the ride of forty or fifty miles she tossed me at least a garbage bag full of revelations, all of them nonsense. At the end of the ride she thrust at me a five dollar bill and told me to get a "really good" meal. As I snatched the bill from her—with protestations of reluctance, of course—I swear that the woman's born-again dog in the back seat gave me a wink.

I went into the restaurant where she had parked, bought myself a cup of coffee, and made a mental reservation to spend the rest of the money on beer and to steal a Gideon's Bible.

After a series of nondescript rides, I was finally picked up by a ridee of some interest, a development that might lead to a radical change in both my plans and itinerary. Said ridee is a priest on vacation who plans to spend several days exploring and "rediscovering" ghost towns of Northern California and Nevada.

Apparently impressed by my wide but shallow knowledge of the Old West, the priest suggested that I might consider accompanying him on his safari. And I might do just that! The guy seems legit and is this night spending the night in the manse of the local parish priest who lives two blocks down the street from the modest inn in which I am ensconced.

I am to meet the good *padre* for breakfast in the morning and discuss the matter further. Right now I shall sally forth for a bite to eat and spend my born-again money (as I did already steal a bible, thank the Lord!)

Friday, August 9, 1996

I arose, thank the Lord or somebody, and after the usual morning ablutions, did keep my rendezvous at the restaurant with my adventurous *padre*. The *padre*, a certain Father Tom Dupree, came along shortly with one Monsignor Murphy and we proceeded to discuss plans over a half-baked breakfast.

In the end, my decision was to go off with Father Tom. Our take-off point: Downieville, California. From thence, we would visit some fifteen to twenty abandoned mining towns as far east as Elko, Nevada, before Father Tom returned to his pastoral duties in Dalles, Oregon, and I staggered into the sunrise of Wisconsin to check on the cattle, mow the lawn, and, most importantly, take care of feeding my beloved spouse of fifty-two years, a woman I love dearly.

Take off we finally did, in a heavy-duty jeep laden with topographic maps and aerial pictures of various ghostly places.

Our initial investigations were north of Downieville, California, where there was supposed to have been some mining camps. We found nothing new, at least that he could authenticate, but then he didn't expect to find much this side of the Sierras.

As evening approached and we were near Downieville, we put up at a modest motel in that same town, the same motel which had, incidentally, sheltered Mother and I some ten or twelve years ago.

As I write this, the good *padre* is walking across the street leading man's best friend—in this case, a six-pack of cold beer. After taking care of that little duty I shall go forth and look the town over. I am told that there are quite a few miners still working the streams around here, most of them old timers, as a hobby, and some of them, Chinese, for a living. That being the case, there should be some characters about.

The *padre* intends to spend the evening drawing up his notes for his next meeting of ghostwriters.

And so this ends the day.

Was aroused by the *padre* a bit early—6:00 AM—but he had his plans...

After coffee we set off in search of lost ghost towns. It seems there were many mining camps that flourished in the area circa 1865-1885 of which there is now no record. Some of these would require almost an archeological dig to find, but then we ghost writers are a dedicated lot.

Our first stop drew a blank; the *padre* thinks his calculations or coordinates were wrong. The next stop, Jack Town, located about fifty miles northeast of Reno, was one he had already explored. Situated at the terminus of a long four-wheel track, Jack Town was a most impressive petrifaction of twelve to fourteen derelict cabins (with evidence of board walks as well) that the *padre* says were built in 1868-1871.

The actual mining in this place was done below the town, on a swift little stream but flash floods, it seems, have wiped out almost all evidence. Nonetheless, the *padre* did manage to find some broken bottles and a worn out shovel which he lovingly labeled and stored in the jeep.

As a result of a giant forest and brush fire on the upper reaches of the Trukee River, a prime place for lost mining camps, our next stops were aborted. But, no mind, the *padre* had ready a fallback plan.

Proceeding with the plan, we stopped first at one known ghost town, an interesting place, and then at another potential sight, but there was nothing to be found.

As the hour was getting late we headed for a little woebegone place, one known only to God and the *padre*, which I now find myself in. The place has only three or four buildings but there were a couple of rooms for rent.

There's no hot water and no telephone and while I would have preferred to camp on the desert, the *padre* had been here before and feels sorry for the faded old harridan who apparently owns the whole shebang.

And so these old ghosters will bed down in most ghostly conditions.

Sunday, August 11, 1996

Awoke early in our primitive habitation, went down to the old harridan's establishment, and partook of what passed for coffee and toast. Thereafter we took off towards Carson City with a stop at a place called Honey Lake where several silver camps were established in 1865-1875.

We found one such place, fairly intact and well known to the *padre* from previous excursions, but were unable to find the others.

It being Sunday we did celebrate an extremely abbreviated mass outside in a most ghostly desert, and then went on to Carson City where the *padre* had some business to attend to at the historical society where he is well known.

We later made another stop at a fairly intact deserted and derelict camp which was interesting to me but old hat to the *padre*.

We are now at an extremely isolated outpost of the B.L.M., the Bureau of Land Management, manned by a young ranger (or whatever they call them) and his wife. There is a telephone which, I've been told, I am free to use with my calling card. And so I will try to call home or, more likely, the home of Kathleen or Maureen, to find out where in hell Mother is. After that it will be the open desert for the night. As the *padre* is well equipped with overnight gear and rations, there is no worry, but the temperature here now is 104 degrees, as it has been for the last four days.

Monday, August 12, 1996

I didn't manage to make any phone calls last night but did spend the night under the stars, fairly comfortable, in the *padre's* blankets. Unfortunately the heavens were obscured by smoke from fires to the west.

After a cold breakfast from the *padre's* jeep and hot coffee from the park ranger's stove, we then set off to the east and north to complete our researches into towns not even ghostly really but are merely suspected to have existed.

We did find two such towns with little trouble, both of which were well preserved. The third town we located was found only after considerable bumping across the desert; unfortunately it had already been thoroughly scavenged. We didn't find much of anything except two old and empty whiskey bottles, a find which tickled the *padre* pink. I suggested they would have been much more interesting if full.

At about 3:00 P.M. we started towards Wells, Nevada, the site of a rendezvous with two other groups of ghost writers, and arrived there about 4:30. The others groups arrived somewhat later and are now with the *padre* comparing notes and pictures. Together they're also dating a whole treasure trove of whiskey bottles and, most important it seems, a couple of wooden doll bodies which would indicate that the camp in which they were found had some women and children.

I will try to call Mother and then have a bite to eat and go to bed. It is 101 degrees outside.

Tuesday, August 13, 1996

Slept the sleep of the just and awoke to find the *padre* working on his notes.

After the usual morning ablutions, packing, and settling of accounts with the *padre*—I probably didn't mention that, at Father Tom's insistence, we had agreed to split expenses, other than transportation—I joined him and the other two groups of ghosters for breakfast.

The group was most erudite and the conversation very enjoyable, but then it was back to the road, Highway 80 in Wells, Nevada.

Things went bad, damned bad, for about two hours. There were no rides and the temperature was creeping towards 100. I believe my problems were due to the fact that a pair of scroungy looking creatures—a he and a she, complete with sleeping bags— had stationed themselves just down the road, a disgusting breech of hitchhiking etiquette.

I was about the repair to the nearest air-conditioned pub and either recast my plan of attack or wait for the pair to give up or be picked up by the local garbage truck but, as ever, in the life of hitchhikers, it is always darkest just before dawn and, at this time of crisis in my career, a fellow stopped to offer me a ride. My benefactor was driving a large new pickup with a fifth-wheel trailer, all new and loaded with two "classic" cars: two 1968 Edsels in mint condition.

After feeling each other out, a ritual of life on the road, we found ourselves compatible and laid bare our souls or, rather, our destinations. His was Detroit and as he was most anxious to have my company, I was most anxious to provide it. And so merrily we rolled to the East.

My companion is a dealer and hauler of classic cars and we stopped along the way at several little desert towns to forage for this kind of merchandise. The area, it seems, its a prime site for them due to its boom-and-bust economy in the 1950s and 1960s and the fact that its climate retards deterioration. He purchased two cars, one in Utah and one in Nevada, to be picked up at a later time.

We stopped for the night—11:00 P.M.—at a large truck stop in eastern Utah. My driver, "General George Marshall"— As that is his given name, you can guess when he was born! — slept in the capacious sleeper of his rig.

I tried to sleep in the seat but with little luck and so spent some of the next five or six hours in the truck stop drinking coffee and reading. Most of the time there, however, was spent talking, or mostly listening, to long-haul truck drivers. Their accents, vocabulary, sense of values, camaraderie, and tales of *past* domesticity made the night seem but short. I think someone should write his Ph.D. thesis on this particular culture—and I might very well do it myself twenty or thirty years from now.

We were back on the road at about 8:00 A.M. and traveling East—Go, go, go!—through Utah, Wyoming, Nebraska, and Iowa. I had intended to part company with the General at Des Moines, then go north to Hwy. 90 and on to Mauston or Richland Center, but because of the Iowa State Fair and some race meet being held in the area there were no motels available. And so we went further East.

We got to Iowa City at midnight and I found myself a room

at Econo-Lodge, an over-priced, extremely run-down gyp joint. Don't ever stop at one.

There I parted company with the General, a truly enjoyable traveling companion.

I know that this crummy hostelry will be a hell of a place to start from in the morning but, as Earl Paul always said, "I suspected the game was crooked but it was the only game in town."

And so I shall go to bed.

Wednesday, August 14, 1996

I arose as one must—late, very late—and surveyed various ways out of the rat trap of roads I had found myself in. The outlook was dismal and I was so sad that I damned near wept. But girding my trusty sword I did sally forth to the battle of getting from here to there.

Fortunately, at a gas station where I stopped to ask directions, the man I questioned said that he himself was going in my direction and could offer me a ride. And so he did get me out of a traffic situation that was most confusing.

After numerous adventures and misadventures I arrived in Lancaster, Wisconsin, and though it was but 4:00 P.M. I decided to stop at a little motel as it was very doubtful that I could finish the journey before dark.

The little inn turned out to be not only the last overnight rest stop in some four to six thousand miles but the cleanest, nicest, and cheapest place I stayed in the entire trip.

Thursday, August 15, 1996

Left late and had a frustrating time; rides were frequent but short and it was not until after some ten or twenty rides that I found

157

myself in Richland Center. At that point I had yet to travel probably less than one half of one percent of the total number of miles of my trip. And so, I stuck up my trusty and well worn thumb and the first vehicle to pick me up was being driven by Ralph Kraemer, our soft-water man, who henceforth drove and deposited me at my very front door where I was welcomed by my aged and most lovable spouse, Annie, and our granddaughter Katie.

I now look forward to a cold beer and a hot meal, and then to lay this powerful frame to rest next to the aforementioned spouse.

And so ends the odyssey of this 20th century A.D. Odysseus.

An Old Man's Rules for Hitchhiking

(through the deserts of the USA and similar regions of the World)

The thought occurs to me that the reminiscences of one of the last dedicated and successful hitchhikers should not be lost to posterity. Hitchhiking is, after all, both an art and a science and should be taught in all public schools. I suppose, however, that some damned do-gooder would say that such a course is contrary to common sense and, therefore, illegal. (In my opinion the lowest form of animal life is the self-appointed do-gooder.) Nonetheless, I shall risk prosecution, much in the spirit of Marco Polo, who wrote the tale of his own travel to and from China and his residence therein while in jail on charges connected with hitchhiking on a camel. And so I shall begin to put down a few of my thoughts as well as some of the commandments and rules on the ancient art of getting from here to there.

These notes were written at the end of the summer of 1996 following a trip to the Western United States. On that particular trip I encountered a smaller percentage of phonies on the road than usual. When searching for the reason I could only conclude that with that both major political parties and Perot's rump party holding, or about to hold, their conventions in San Diego, Chicago, or wherever, all the real first-class phonies were at those points or converging on them, thus leaving the open road to the interesting and honest bum.

On a final note I would like to tell anyone who cares to listen that if there's something you want to do or some place you dream of going, for God's sake do it before you die. But when you get out that on the road, don't be surprised what people think. I find that about eighty percent of your ridees' first impression of an aged wanderer will be that you are slightly off your rocker. After engaging in conversation with the ridee, about the same percentage secretly envy you and wish they had the originality to do it themselves. Of course, among family members and small-town friends, the percentage is probably between ninety-seven and ninety-nine percent.

BEGINNER'S RULES

1. Be old.

   This will take time.

2. Be alone.

   Always follow this commandment. And not only should you be alone on the road—No one in his right mind will pick up a caravan and you don't want to be caught in a car with a real loony—you should also be alone in the world, a widower, preferably. While one of God's rule may be to not tell lies, a lie as defined by this ancient hitchhiker does not quite cover entertainment.

   As to the cause of your widower-hood, it should vary with the age and gender of your ridee. If the ridee is a woman or an elderly couple, a traumatic separation from your beloved spouse is best: "A week before our golden wedding my beloved spouse was picking roses from her well-tended garden and fell victim to the attack of an un-suspected nest of killer bees therein. I am now traveling to try to forget the hellish memory..." Such a tear jerker is usually good for a lift through the ridee's town of destination, a recommendation as to the best and cheapest lodging, and probably a cup of coffee. Your story will make ridees feel fortunate that their own lives have not been tinged with such tragedy and will put them in a generous mood.

In case of a more calloused ridee—a middle-aged semi-retired truck driver or construction worker, for instance, whose work takes him thousands of miles from home base (and who is likely to have been married several times)—a different story is advised, one stressing hardship over happiness. Try something along these lines: you worked hard and with the help of your late and beloved spouse raised and educated a large family. Then, just when you were about to retire and travel and take it easy, lo and behold, your "old lady" fell victim to a debilitating disease. After several years of your devoted care, she did finally go to that pasture in the sky but left you at loose ends, living on a small pension—your savings and estate having been wiped out by medical racketeers.

This sad rigmarole usually warms up your ridee and reassures him as to the wisdom of his course: several marriages, minimal domesticity, and the mirage of future happiness. Indeed, for the adult male hitchhiker, the grieving widower is the most sympathetic role. Even the most cynical ridee will go an extra mile for such a sad character.

3. Be clean.

   This is essential. As to how to remain clean, one suggestion that almost never fails is, about every fourth night, arrange to bivouac in a smallish prairie or desert town, one large enough to have a Laundromat and small enough to be friendly. After pitching camp (in probably the only hotel or motel in town) gather together all soiled clothes and at about 7:00 P.M., while looking your oldest and most dignified, head for the washery. At said washery you will probably find a group of women doing their washing. Look helpless as the devil and ask some fifty-ish looking woman how to operate the washing machines. Almost inevitably the woman's companions will gather 'round and you will then have a large pool of willing help.

   You might mention that your recently departed wife always did such things and, *ergo*, they will take over: they'll wash and press your clothes and send you on your way.

4. Travel light.

   Luggage should consist of as small a case as practical but one strong enough to sit on in case you're caught out in the desert where traffic is sparse.

   As to the contents of said case, aside from what you're wearing, the essentials for one old man would be:
   - two light-colored, stylish trousers (Make sure they're washable!);
   - three light-colored, but not white, shirts;
   - two pair of under-shorts;
   - four pair of socks;
   - two disposable razors (Remember, you might lose one.)

162

- one extra comb;
- one wind-breaker or other light jacket;
- half your traveling funds, either in the form of; travelers' checks or cash;
- matches;
- if you smoke, extra tobacco;
- a small flashlight;
- a toothbrush;
- maps (A good map is essential.)

In regard to footwear, wear comfortable thick-soled shoes as the roads in the desert get hotter than hell. As for head gear, a cap is a necessity. Wear a light colored cap with the logo of some venerable organization such as the Elks, the American Legion, the VFW, or whatever. Such a little thing as that will, from time to time, yield one an extra hundred miles or so.

5. Have a general knowledge of both the area in which you're traveling and any other destination you might have. This knowledge will enable you to make better conversation with the ridee.

6. When using the thumb, always pick out a place on the road where the ridee has a clear view of you. Try to make especially sure the sun is not in the ridee's eyes. For that reason:
    - When traveling West, try for an early morning start and an early evening stop as the sun will be in the ridee's eyes the entire day.
    - When traveling East, try to find a spot shaded by a hill, a mountain, or a north-south jog.

- When traveling North-South, place yourself in an extended area of shade or sunlight. It is also advisable to wear your lightest colored clothes.

7. After studying traffic patterns, angle of the sun, width of the road's shoulder, and ease of stopping for the ridee, stick to your spot. (He who walks is a damned fool.)

8. Tis always best to stand on an up-slope as the heavy trucks will be forced to slow down, making it easier for the cars behind to stop.

9. Stand partially facing your potential ridee so that he can see your mien. Further in this regard, always present a cheerful face and wave back at any driver who waves at you. Not seldom will the driver be impressed, go down the road a ways, make a U-turn, return to where you're standing, make another U-turn, and pick you up. Such a ride will usually be a long one.

10. If at all possible let the ridee strike up the conversation first. This gives you a chance to sort of feel out what sort of bugger the ridee is.

11. Once conversation has begun try to make yourself entertaining but use impeccable English. This never fails to impress the educated and to awe the semi-literate.

    Conversation with ridees and, for that matter, anybody else who cares to listen, is very important. "Conversation" not only determines the pleasure of a ride; it can also determine the length of the ride as well.

INTERMEDIATE RULES

While the Hitchhiking Commandments constitute a general guide for getting one's foot inside the door of a vehicle, once you've actually been given a lift there are a couple more rules to follow:

12. As noted in Commandment 10, first allow the ridee to develop the line of conversation. Once you have established rapport with him, adjust your conversation to his. If he's a man of the world be his equal in philosophy, conversation, and, above all, in vocabulary.

    Based on my experience about ninety percent of ridees are above average in terms of both vocabulary and experience. Eventually some subject will arise of which you are clearly more informed than your ridee. Take advantage of this opening and use it to impress them, but don't overdo it. No one likes a smart aleck.

    If, as will happen from time to time, your ridee turns out to be really stupid or prejudiced, adjust your conversation to somewhat above his level. If you start agreeing with him he'll think that you're a real gem of a man—in short, stupid and prejudiced too. Once again, if the ridee is stupid—And I use the male pronoun because 80% of your hosts are likely to be male—try to be slightly less stupid.

    Finally, never lie unless it's convenient to do so and then make it entertaining.

13. Try to have the ridee reveal his or her destination and itinerary before you reveal yours. That way, if the ridee says he's just going down the road forty miles and then turning south to Mexico City, you can say that's exactly where you are headed. You might not really want to go there but never pass up a three thousand mile ride, whether it be to Mexico, Alaska, or Timbuktu.

14. If your ridee turns out to be a religious or political nut do not agree with him; hint, however, that you might be open to conversion. In most cases such a person will take you clear through his town of destination and possibly even buy you a meal just, I think, to keep a captive audience.

15. Should a uniformed minion of the law pull up beside you with the obvious attention of asserting his authority, smile at him and say something like, "I sure would be grateful and most thankful, sir, if you were to assist me in getting away from this local traffic." Chances are said minion will react like a snarling dog when petted: wiggle his tail, give you a ride out of town, and deposit you at a spot advantageous to further travel.

There are many more words of wisdom that I am capable of giving but the ones jotted down are probably more than either the novice or intermediate hitchhiker might be willing or able to digest. For the more intrepid traveler, however, I offer further thoughts and advice to the tyro ground bound albatross.

GRADUATE STUDIES

I, having had some little experience in being alone in a land of a completely different language know that this situation is a challenge to test the steel of any wayfarer. Nonetheless, it is really not as fearful as one would think. Firstly, all people are basically the same, whether they are white, black, red or yellow; whether they live in a palace, a hogan in the desert, an igloo in the far north, or in a hobo jungle. All have their own language but there's a certain instinctive sign language by which you can communicate—and I do mean instinctive. First, and most important, is facial expression. Both a smile and a frown are instinctive and cannot be taught or learned. Next is hand signals. An upturned palm seems to be an instinctive sign of friendship—or surrender. Others are obvious. Hunger: pat your belly and then point at your mouth. For some reason in most cultures pointing with your finger arouses suspicion and is almost considered an insult. As to why, I do not know, but don't do it.

I have had some little experience along this line on my own volition: the length and breadth of Mexico; likewise French speaking Quebec; the Creole area of southern Louisiana; the teeming waterfronts of Indonesia; and the slums of Panama City and Puerto Rico. Add to this, under the pressure of the necessity of war, I crossed a bit of Germany, all of France, and a good bit of Spain, not really hitchhiking but existing for three months in lands of language completely foreign to me. But still the instinctive and universal language (along with the care of the French Underground during The War) made travel possible and almost enjoyable. Enough of this polemic and back to a few additional rules.

16. While traveling in the Old South don't be too politically correct—a red neck is a red neck and a bleeding heart do gooder will forever be the same. There seems to be no middle ground. (Although for some reason the fact that I had a grandfather and two great grandfathers in the Union Army who were part of Sherman's Army in his march from Atlanta to the sea seems to elicit a sort of sense of camaraderie—a perverse sort of attitude that's beyond me.)

17. While traveling by thumb in the east, try to stay in or near the Appalachians. The people there have known and probably still know poverty but once you get beneath their

outer crust, which is hard, they are the most generous and entertaining people you can find.

18. As to places to avoid, first and foremost: newly developed resorts for the newly rich. There is only one class more arrogant and greedy than those of old, inherited wealth and that is the newly rich, their wealth acquired by quasi-legal thievery and, in all probability, war profiteering. Probably the only difference between old and new rich is two or three generations and the old rich have gone to "better" schools and have had more time to polish their arrogance and to practice the more exotic forms of depravity. Especially avoid Colorado ski resorts. The denizens of these tinsel imitation Swiss chalets are insufferable, interested in only impressing their own kind and scheming to add to their wealth by stealing from the poor. The formerly friendly locals have been so corrupted that they regard any wayfarer as a potential victim rather than a character who might prove friendly and interesting. I did one day hear one new rich woman, on being asked in the beauty shop if she cared for a shampoo, reply with the haughty answer, "I'll have you know that we are rich enough and I'll have nothing but genuine poos."

Naturally, another place to avoid is resort areas of the "old" rich. The arrogant creatures inhabiting these places have learned how to insult and rob you in a more genteel manner than the new rich.

But this blasted pen does run on too long and so does this old man's reminisces. Did just think of one more rather esoteric hitchhiking trip, that of traversing the vast Indian lands of the southwest and to some extent of the Dakotas, Montana, and

Wyoming. There's a story in it that illustrates the last and, possibly, most golden rule of hitchhiking, namely that when in Rome you do as the Romans do. No matter where you find yourself, you must always bare in mind that you are in a completely different culture from your own and must respect it. Using my trip in the Indian lands as an example, you must remember that the Native Americans have a somewhat different set of values than we, who in spite of different ethnic and religious backgrounds, have for generations been with the so called "Protestant Ethic"— a concept completely foreign to them and rightly so. If you treat these gentle people with respect, the first one who picks you up will, it seems, pass you on to someone going your direction, each ridee regarding you, it seems, as a brother. There is no hurry, and when it's time to sleep, you sleep. On that trip I did spend two nights in sheepherders' "hogans" and we men did sit, talk, eat, and sip on a short supply of beer. The women and kids seemed to do all the herding and cooking—a high form of civilization it seems to me.

After some three and a half days of leisurely travel in this awesome landscape, I did arrive with my fourteen or so brothers at the perimeter of their land, in Flagstaff, Arizona, I believe it was. As is the custom of this culture, I pressed a gift on my departing "brother," a case of beer, and it was well received. I was invited— sincerely invited—to return at any time. I hope that chance and time allows it.

I get the feeling that if you showed up in Indian territory and put on the do-gooder-reformer-missionary act you would be completely shunned, and with good reason. They regard all of those mentioned above as land thieves, murderers, and deceivers of the lowest degree. The past proves their conception correct.

169

The point of this last little tale is to know the land you're in—it doesn't matter whether it's Indonesia, Mexico, or some other part of the United States—and respect the denizens of those regions. It is their land and just as you would not want someone coming on to your property and telling you what to do, much less cheating you out of it in some low-down deceitful way, you must abide by local rules. You don't have to like them, but you do have to respect them.

But enough, dear children, of these ramblings. Don't expect them earth shaking, but some of you or your descendants might some day come across them in some old family junk pile and find them of some interest. Until then I bid you a fond adieu.

www.ingramcontent.com/pod-product-compliance
Lightning Source LLC
Chambersburg PA
CBHW021231090426
42740CB00006B/476